LA MESA CAMPESINA

LA MESA CAMPESINA

A Congregational Resource for Ministry with Migrant and Agricultural Farmworkers

by
THELMA HERRERA FLORES

WIPF & STOCK · Eugene, Oregon

LA MESA CAMPESINA
A Congregational Resource for Ministry with Migrant and Agricultural Farmworkers

Copyright © 2024 Thelma Herrera Flores. All rights reserved. Except for brief quotations in critical publications or reviews, no part of this book may be reproduced in any manner without prior written permission from the publisher. Write: Permissions, Wipf and Stock Publishers, 199 W. 8th Ave., Suite 3, Eugene, OR 97401.

Wipf & Stock
An Imprint of Wipf and Stock Publishers
199 W. 8th Ave., Suite 3
Eugene, OR 97401

www.wipfandstock.com

PAPERBACK ISBN: 979-8-3852-1052-7
HARDCOVER ISBN: 979-8-3852-1053-4
EBOOK ISBN: 979-8-3852-1054-1

06/12/24

Scripture quotations are from New Revised Standard Version Bible, copyright © 1989, National Council of Churches of Christ in the United States of America. Used by permission. All rights reserved worldwide.

Excerpts from *Y No se lo Tragó la Tierra* by Tomás Rivera reprinted by permission from the publisher (© 1987 Arte Público Press - University of Houston).

"Vamos Todos al Banquete / Let Us Go Now to the Banquet" from *Misa Popular Salvadoreña* by Guillermo Cuéllar, English translation by Bret Hesla and William Dexheimer Pharris. Copyright © 1998, trans. © 1996 GIA Publications, Inc. All rights reserved. Used by permission.

I dedicate my book to my husband, Rev. Dr. Daniel F. Flores, my family, and many friends. A special feeling of gratitude to my affectionate and adoring husband and best friend whose words of encouragement and push for tenacity ring in my ears. Thank you for believing in me. I love you.

To my "little momma," Margarita J. Herrera, and my brother, Rev. Joel J. Herrera, for their interest and curiosity in my project and for the weekly phone calls to check on my progress. Thank you for your support. I love you both.

I also dedicate this work to my many friends and church family who have sustained me with their prayers throughout the entire doctorate process. I appreciate you.

Contents

Acknowledgments | ix

Preface | xi

Chapter 1
Campesinos in America | 1

Chapter 2
Towards a Campesino Theology | 19

Chapter 3
Reading to Understand Campesinos | 38

Chapter 4
Teaching about Campesinos | 57

Chapter 5
Reaching Campesinos | 84

    Appendix A: Jimenez Produce Truck | 95

    Appendix B: *Tijeras* (Single Spring) | 96

    Appendix C: *Tijeras* (Double Spring) | 97

    Appendix D: Short-Handled Hoe | 98

    Appendix E: Hand Sickle | 99

    Appendix F: Hand Scale | 100

    Appendix G: Popeye Statue | 101

Appendix H: Cesar Chavez Meeting with Hispanic Methodists in Fort Worth | 102

Appendix I: *Campesino* Camp Prayer Circle | 103

Appendix J: *Campesino* Welcome Kit | 104

Appendix K: "Vamos Todos al Banquete" | 105

Appendix L: Curriculum Lesson Plans | 106

Appendix M: *Bittersweet Harvest* Posters | 117

Appendix N: Class Session Six | 118

Appendix O: *Campesina* Seder Plate | 119

Appendix P: *La Mesa Campesina Fiesta* | 120

Appendix Q: "De Colores" | 121

Appendix R: H.R.1603—Farm Workforce Modernization Act of 2021 | 122

Appendix S: Advocacy Visit to Office of US Senator Ted Cruz | 124

Bibliography | 125

Acknowledgments

THIS RESOURCE IS THE PRODUCT of my doctoral studies at Western Theological Seminary in Holland, Michigan. I wish to thank my committee members who were generous with their time and expertise. Thank you to my committee chairman, Dr. Alvin Padilla, for his leadership in the Doctor of Ministry program. His foresight in intentionally selecting a diverse group of students for this cohort was a rich blessing.

Thanks to Dr. Hector Ortiz for his countless hours of reading, reflecting, and encouraging, and most of all for his patience throughout the entire process.

I am grateful to the publishers who granted permission to reprint portions of copyrighted material. Portions of my doctoral proposal previously published in *Los Profetas: The Prophetic Role of Hispanic Churches in America*, Wesley's Foundery Press, 2022, are included in this book with improvements and expansions. Many thanks to Wipf & Stock's editing team Emily Callihan, Jonathan Hill, and Shannon Carter.

Finally, I want to acknowledge and thank my church family at La Trinidad United Methodist Church (Seguin) and Pastor Nohemí Ramirez for allowing me to conduct my research project with the Wednesday night Bible study group. Their excitement and willingness to participate made the completion of my research an enjoyable experience.

Preface

THE PURPOSE OF THIS RESOURCE is to develop an ecumenical ministry with Hispanic migrant and seasonal agricultural workers, also known as *Campesinos,* in the United States of America. The *Campesinos* encounter numerous struggles that go beyond the poverty of living standards, food, and education. This study will address a specific problem within the communities of *Campesinos.* Namely, I am concerned with the lack of spiritual leadership and guidance by clergy and laypersons to this population.

This educational resource is designed to enable churches to understand the plight of the *Campesinos* through Bible study, testimonials, watching selected portions of videos, singing, and sharing fellowship *Campesino* meals. The purpose is to stir up the church's heart to action and lead them to a hands-on ministry with the migrant agricultural farmworkers.

It is my hope that my own United Methodist Church and her ecumenical partners will reach out to the *Campesinos* to help them discover that Christ is walking next to them in the crop rows and drinking with them from the irrigation ditches. I believe in the beauty manifested through God's love. This same love allows us to see that we are all the same. We all need Jesus.

Chapter 1

Campesinos in America

THIS STUDY FOCUSES ON developing ministry with Hispanic migrant and seasonal agricultural workers in the United States of America. It is comprised of five chapters. In the first chapter, I discuss the perceived problem within my ministry context. The second chapter highlights the biblical and theological foundations for a practical *Campesino* theology. In the third chapter, we will explore resources for understanding *Campesinos*. The fourth chapter focuses on the practice of teaching about *Campesinos*. The fifth chapter will culminate our discussion with a call to reach *Campesinos*.

Chapter 1, as previously stated, provides an overview of my ministry context and the observed problem, which is a lack of spiritual presence, leadership, and guidance by my denomination, the United Methodist Church. From my first-hand observations, the United Methodist Church has not been able to provide a viable and sustainable ministry with Hispanic migrant and seasonal agricultural workers locally, regionally, or nationally. This ministry of compassion is Wesleyan insomuch as it fits John Wesley's description of "works of mercy" in Sermon 98, "On Works of Mercy."[1] Such ministry involving *Campesinos* has yet to be visualized and realized within the United Methodist Church in North America.

---

1. Wesley, *Works*, 384.

La Mesa Campesina

MINISTRY CONTEXT

My familiarity and concern for migrant workers is a direct result of my *Campesino* heritage. I was born into a family of *Campesinos*. Field workers who provide the labor for sowing, cultivating and harvesting are known in the agricultural community as *Campesinos*. They are the "invisible" people who harvest the fields of all their bounty without much recognition by society or the church. Yet, *Campesinos* are necessary to feed the world. As a deacon with *Campesino* roots, I feel called to feed them the word of God.

I was born in Crystal City, Texas. It is a predominantly Mexican American migrant agricultural town in South Texas located near the border of Mexico. Because of its mild winters and abundant sunshine, crops are grown year-round. Historically, the crop of choice was spinach. Crystal City was known as "the spinach capital of the world." Spinach was such a lucrative crop it was referred to as "green gold" by the all-Anglo city leaders.[2] In 1937, these same city leaders commissioned and erected a shiny fiberglass statue of Popeye which was placed in front of city hall. This statue, however, was interpreted differently by the Anglo and Mexican heritage residents. For the Anglo city leaders, Popeye symbolized a source of prosperity for a thriving spinach industry. But for the Mexicans, the statue represented the cycle of poverty. "'We hated that statue,' said Jose Angel Gutierrez . . . 'The statue symbolized our servitude to the spinach and the Anglo owners of the company.'"[3]

When World War II broke out in the 1940s, fewer Mexican migrants were coming from the Northwest and the Midwest states of the USA because of a fear of being arrested. The few migrants that lived in the migrant camp built for them in Crystal City were booted out to make room for imprisoned US citizens. The United States government repurposed the migrant camp into a multinational family internment camp. The family camp in Crystal City housed Japanese, German, and Italian heritage Americans who

---

2. Russell, *Train to Crystal City*, 41.
3. Russell, *Train to Crystal City*, 42.

had been designated by the government as "enemy aliens." Years later, this internment camp became my elementary school. This is where I attended kindergarten through third grade before my family moved to San Antonio, Texas. It is important to note that public education in Crystal City was also ground zero for Hispanic political activism with La Raza Unida Party in the 1970s.[4]

My grandparents, parents, and mother-in-law were all *Campesinos*. My family understood and shared stories with me about the harsh conditions associated with picking cotton in the hot Texas sun. My father, Alfonso Herrera, would often speak of what it was like to harvest asparagus in Minnesota and Michigan. He grew to dread the early morning shadow of those "little soldiers" that, according to him, would grow overnight. After the daily harvest, they would reappear the next day as if they were never touched.

I remember, as a child of about five years of age, my grandfather took me with him one day to work in the fields to pick watermelons. My grandfather, Enrique Jimenez, was a foreman. He owned a big yellow school bus which he used for picking up the fieldworkers from their homes throughout Crystal City. My grandmother, Herminia, would rise at 3:00 a.m. to prepare and pack his breakfast and lunch of freshly made flour tortilla tacos and fill his thermos with fresh hot coffee. She did this before setting off to work herself at 4:30 a.m. at the Del Monte cannery. Enrique would start driving his bus route between four and five o'clock in the morning, ensuring arrival at the watermelon field before six. Of course, I was too young to do any actual work. My only task consisted of rolling one watermelon from the field to the collection site. I mainly played and sat in the shade of the big yellow bus. From that vantage point, I could watch the laborers going up and down each of the furrows. First, one crew would go through and cut the watermelons from the vines. Then another crew would follow and harvest them. It was not until years later I realized what was fun for me was quite the opposite for those individuals who

---

4. Gutiérrez, *Making of a Chicano Militant*, and Navarro, *Cristal Experiment*, 1998.

clocked extremely long hours of backbreaking work. They spent the entire day stooping over as they harvested the watermelons. The *Campesinos'* only break was when they stopped to drink some water and eat a quick lunch of homemade taquitos. At the end of the week, I noticed the laborers lining up outside my grandfather's front door. I asked my grandfather why all the people were gathering outside. He told me these were his workers, and they were there to collect their wages for the work they had done. I asked if I too could get paid. He answered in the affirmative if indeed I had worked. I did work. After all, I had single-handedly harvested a watermelon. That week I earned twenty-five cents!

Some of my memories of *Campesino* life were firsthand and others were communicated to me by my family. My relatives knew what it was like to travel from South Texas to *el Norte*—Michigan, Minnesota, and Wisconsin. Sometimes they rode in the bed of a truck or on top of freshly harvested crops. To this day my mother, Margarita, hates the smell of onions because of those long truck rides with sacks of onions. My relatives recognized from personal experience the bitter and painful reality of a *Campesino*'s life. Their days were marked by fear and insecurity resulting in a life without hope. Like many *Campesinos* today, they existed without knowing God's promise to harvesters as depicted in Isaiah.

> They shall feed along the ways, on all the bare trails shall be their pasture; they shall not hunger or thirst, neither scorching wind nor sun shall strike them down, for he who has pity on them will lead them, and by springs of water will guide them.[5]

I believe it is our responsibility as members of the church to offer the *Campesinos* the hope of God's grace. Hope is born when the beloved community is energized by God's presence in our lives, even in the most difficult circumstances.

My ministry context is with Hispanic migrant and seasonal agricultural workers in Texas. In recent years, the mass media has appropriated the term "migrant" to refer to people who enter the

---

5. Isa 49:9–10.

country without authorization, typically at the southern US-Mexico border. The National Agricultural Workers Survey (NAWS) has defined a migrant as "a person who reported jobs that were at least 75 miles apart or who reported moving more than 75 miles to obtain a farm job during a 12-month period."[6] In this study, I will use the term "migrant" only to refer to US-based laborers who migrate to harvest crops outside of their home region or state. For example, agricultural workers who migrate from their homes in Texas to harvest blueberries in Michigan are considered "migrants." Seasonal agricultural workers often reside near the general area of the farms and fields where they work. An exception is the H2A visa workers who enter the US legally and return to their home country after the harvest. I will use the umbrella term *Campesinos* to refer to all populations of migrant and seasonal agricultural workers throughout this study.

My ministry involvement with *Campesinos* began in Ottawa County in West Michigan. Many of these laborers hail from Texas. The majority of these *Campesinos* work in nurseries and blueberry fields. They are part of a larger group that travels to Michigan annually from Florida, Georgia, Tennessee, and Texas. It was a common practice of farmers to advance travel money to their Texas workers so they would arrive in Michigan indebted to them.[7] Many live in substandard housing labor camps provided by the farmers or their agents. As I met and interacted with the *Campesinos* at the labor camps I had the opportunity to witness their living conditions. At one camp, housing was provided in big red barns. Each barn was divided into two areas of living quarters. Each lodging area was partitioned into four mini-apartments. The barns were equipped with a common cooking and eating area that included picnic-style tables. Each mini apartment housed four families separated by blankets hung from the ceiling. The *Campesinos* slept on crude makeshift beds on the floor. When I probed about their comfort in the accommodations, they told me that they did not like the over-crowdedness of the apartments. However, most said that it

6. "Findings from the National Agricultural Workers Survey," 7.
7. Prifogle, "Rural Social Safety Nets," 1025.

La Mesa Campesina

was much better than what they had been living in before. The *Campesinos* were grateful for these fairly new barns. Of course, not all accommodations at the various camps were perfect. It is good to know that the State of Michigan has inspectors who periodically visit the camps to evaluate the housing accommodations for health and safety.[8] This state organization manages much more than housing issues. They are present to help with such needs as harassment and compensation issues. An incident of harassment by a Michigan farmer was caught on camera.

> When a Conklin-area grower's son was recently caught on camera spewing racist venom at a group of migrant workers, it was Migrant Legal Aid the worker contacted for assistance. The agency helped the man file a police report, and Ottawa County's prosecutor charged the farmer's son with misdemeanor assault for allegedly spitting on a worker.[9]

My ministry to *Campesinos* in Michigan included collaboration with churches in Fort Worth, Texas. I also benefitted from the in-kind donations and financial support from various churches in Michigan. Several church friends in Fort Worth sent financial support which helped to provide pillows, cookware, groceries, caps, socks, and personal hygiene items. One group of laypeople from the churches in Michigan drove two hours each way to deliver donated supplies. One clergywoman, Rev. Laura Feliciano, who at that time was pastoring La Nueva Esperanza United Methodist Church in Grand Rapids, Michigan, provided me with $2,000's worth of $20 Walmart gift cards. This servant of God requested a grant for her own ministry and was compelled to request help for my ministry with the *Campesinos*. This was indeed a surprise and a blessing! Every one of those gift cards was distributed not only to Hispanic/Latino laborers but also to the Haitian community of blueberry farmworkers in Holland, Michigan. Dr. Margie Crawford, the District Superintendent of the United Methodist Church in Grand Rapids, was also very supportive of this ministry.

8. Samples, "Inside W. Mi Migrant Camps."
9. Samples, "Inside W. Mi Migrant Camps."

Sonya Luna, the Michigan Conference Hispanic Ministry Director, provided funds and made connections for me in the Michigan Conference of the UMC. My ministry was fruitful because of these collaborations. I am convinced that this ministry is most successful when it is done in partnership with other churches and clergy.

My current ministry context is the *Campesinos* of Texas. However, this population's work is intricately connected with Michigan as well as other northern states. Therefore, there are lessons to be gleaned from their out-of-state experiences.

It is unknown exactly how many farmworkers come to Michigan annually. However, the "Migrant and Seasonal Farmworkers Enumeration Profiles Estimate" from 2013 provides the best available data on the total number of farmworkers.[10] Drawing on the data from that report, the table below gives a useful snapshot of the migrant population in Ottawa County as compared to the total in the State of Michigan. According to these estimates, as many as 9084 migrant workers and their families come to Ottawa County annually. The following visualization is indicative of the different groups that make up this large population of *Campesinos*.

---

10. "Migrant and Seasonal Farmworker Enumeration."

La Mesa Campesina

Table A: Migrant and Seasonal Farmworker Enumeration Profiles Estimate 2013[11]

Location in Michigan	MSFW Estimates	Migrant Workers	Seasonal Workers	Non-Farmworkers Migrant Households	Non-Farmworkers Seasonal Households	Total MSFW Workers and non-farm-workers
Ottawa County	6,951	4,754	2,196	4,330	2,065	13,345
State Total	49,135	32,337	16,798	29,227	15,805	94,167

In addition to these state findings, I have observed the following. Most of these laborers are single men. There are also some women and a few families with school-aged or younger children. I have encountered a few middle-aged couples and seniors that were older than the typical age group of twenty-five to thirty-five years old. The low numbers in this older group can probably be attributed to the strain of the long hours of backbreaking work.

Most of these laborers do not have a high school diploma. "The average level of formal education completed by farmworkers was ninth grade."[12] Agricultural work is one of the few types of employment accessible to low-education laborers. *Campesinos* regularly journey from their home in search of a way to provide for their basic physical needs of food and shelter. They are the working poor of our rural communities. Because they are rarely seen in public, they are "invisible." Working in the *piscas*, or harvest fields, is not an unusual scenario for *Campesino* families. It is a tradition within many family groups to pursue this type of work generation after generation. This lifestyle can negatively affect all members of the household and it can become an inescapable generational cyclical pattern: travel—harvest—home. In Texas, school-aged children are pulled out of school in March to travel to the *piscas* to help their parents pick crops in the fields. They often return to

---

11. "Migrant and Seasonal Farmworker Enumeration."
12. "Findings from the National Agricultural Workers Survey," 13.

their schools in the fall after the school year has already begun. All the travel back and forth from home to the farms in various states results in missed months of critical education. Their subsistence labor offers very little opportunity for educational and financial success or upward mobility. Because agricultural work is their primary means of support, it is almost impossible to break from this cyclical existence.

PROBLEM

This study will address a specific problem encountered by *Campesinos* that goes beyond the poverty of living standards, food, and education. They are in serious need of ministry for their spiritual well-being. Although there are many different types of spirituality, the Protestant-Evangelical focus is on a spirituality that leads to a personal relationship with God. This is not to discount the presence of nonreligious spirituality, pseudo-spiritual practices such as meditation, or secular appreciation of nature, art, etc. They are, simply put, not within the scope of study for this research. Many of the religious *Campesinos* are cut off from their spiritual homes because of the distance from their home church and the remoteness of the *piscas*. The faraway locations leave them with little or no spiritual guidance from their pastors or priests. As the *Campesinos* enter their "home away from home," familiarity with their new locale and their lack of transportation from labor camps to churches is a challenge. *Campesinos* typically work six days per week from before sunrise to late in the day after sunset. Their Sabbath rest is at the discretion of the farmer, the nature of the weather, and the abundance and urgency of the harvest. Consequently, they immediately become isolated from any outside spiritual resources. They are dependent on the infrequent outreach and visitation of pastors, priests, laity, and social workers for their spiritual and emotional support. Lacking this support, *Campesinos* struggle for survival with few spiritual resources inside their labor camps.

Eighty years ago, this lack of Spiritual support caught the attention of the Roman Catholic Church. According to Deborah

E. Kanter, Roman Catholics pioneered ministry to *Campesinos* in the middle of the twentieth century.[13] It began in earnest with the Bracero Movement in 1942. The Bracero Program was intended as an emergency wartime effort that recruited men specifically from Mexico to fill the need for temporary agricultural laborers and railroad workers due to World War II. The USA faced a scarcity of manual workers in the essential industries of food and transportation because most men were preoccupied with the struggle of our country's war. What had been envisioned by the USA as a temporary solution to their shortfall became, instead, an industry dependent on these migrant workers.

After World War II, Congress renewed the Bracero Program, which continued until 1964. Archbishop Garibi of Guadalajara, Mexico, observed that "the migrant work in northern states is not decreasing but growing."[14] It is noteworthy that ten thousand Mexican heritage migrants traveled from Texas to Michigan annually.[15] Within a decade that number grew to one hundred forty thousand.[16] It was Archbishop Garibi who first began discussions in 1944 to send Spanish-speaking priests from Mexico to the US to provide ministry to the braceros. Unfortunately, it was not until almost a decade later that Mexican Catholic priests were at long last sent to Michigan. By this time Michigan Catholics had already launched the ministry and laid the foundation for the visiting priests. The priests soon learned that to minister to the braceros they would have to follow the workers as they in turn followed the crops. These bracero-directed priests became itinerating ministers of the gospel. Moreover, each priest had to collaborate with the local parish priest. This is significant because it informs us that the *Campesino* ministry, which is transient, is too large for one

---

13. Kanter, "Mexican Priests."

14. Kanter, "Mexican Priests," 97.

15. Robert E. Lucey, "Analysis of Report by Father Radtke Concerning Migrant Mexican Workers in the North Central States," quoted in Kanter, "Mexican Priests," 97.

16. Dennis Valdés, *Al Norte*, quoted in Kanter, "Mexican Priests," 97.

church to handle on its own. They learned this ministry is best done cooperatively.

Campesino ministry falls into what John Wesley categorized as "works of mercy." Rev. Tom Albin, dean of the Upper Room at the General Board of Discipleship notes, "Wesley considered works of mercy as the concrete expression of love with skin on it."[17] In other words, "works of mercy" includes doing good works such as visiting the sick and imprisoned, feeding the hungry, and giving generously to the needy. Wesley went beyond the physical and emotional needs of the vulnerable community. He believed works of mercy should integrate the care of the spiritual needs of the poor, marginalized, and oppressed.

Campesinos are an especially vulnerable community that can easily be taken advantage of by farmers or be completely forgotten by churches. From my observation and interaction with them, I know they need spiritual leadership and guidance. Many of them desire a pastoral presence. The *Campesinos* hunger to hear God's good word. They want to pray and have prayers lifted on their behalf.

Campesinos need advocacy from the church as well as the state. The State of Michigan has an effective Department of Civil Rights that advocates for justice for migrant and seasonal agricultural workers.[18] The local Migrant Resource Council, a regional division of the Department of Civil Rights, has been very welcoming to faith-based ministries. I have been able to enjoy the company of the Migrant Resource Council and members of churches from different faith traditions as we collaborated to reach the *Campesinos*.

The challenge remains to organize an outreach program led by local churches and clergy to this community. I presented this congregational program focusing on *Campesino* spiritual resources at La Trinidad United Methodist Church in Seguin, Texas. La Trinidad UMC is a 116-year-old church. It is one of three United Methodist churches in Seguin, a small town with a history of racial

---

17. Snell, "Means of Grace."

18. Michigan Department of Health and Human Services, https://www.michigan.gov/mdhhs.

segregation. La Trinidad is the Hispanic church. The other two are Wesley Harper UMC, an African American church, and Walnut Springs United Methodist Church, which is primarily an Anglo congregation. La Trinidad is a small membership church with an average Sunday worship attendance of fifty persons, including children and youth. As a bilingual congregation, the worship services are held in both English and Spanish. Approximately one-half of the congregation is college-educated. About 60 percent of the congregation is over the age of seventy, with most of them closer to eighty and ninety years of age. Several of the members of this church have worked with *Campesinos* in the school district or they themselves have worked in the *piscas*. The community of Seguin is historically known as a *Campesino* sending community. Although my focus is on the *Campesinos* of Texas, one must recognize and acknowledge the interstate nature of *Campesino* work. One state sends *Campesinos* and another receives them. The local churches need to understand their roles in ministering to the specific needs of the *Campesinos* at each end of the journey.

In 2019 the population of Seguin, located in Guadalupe County, was 29,992 with 52 percent Hispanic and 22.5 percent of those Hispanics or Latinos living in poverty. It is noteworthy that the religious composition of Guadalupe County is 16.3 percent Evangelical Protestant, 11.5 percent Catholic, and 5.4 percent Mainline Protestant. These numbers are significant because they reflect that even in a Hispanic-majority community, the number of Protestants is about double the number of Catholics.[19]

HYPOTHESIS

If we do not heed the words of the Gospel of Matthew that clearly outline our mission as Christians "to the least of these," then the church fails in her ministry to the *Campesinos*. Our calling as evidenced by the words of Jesus is to care tenderly, compassionately, and fully for the poor in all their circumstances.

19. City-Data, "Seguin, Texas."

> For I was hungry, and you gave me food,
> I was thirsty and you gave me something to drink,
> I was a stranger and you welcomed me.
> I was naked and you gave me clothing.
> I was sick and you took care of me,
> I was in prison, and you visited me.[20]

The church's treatment of the *Campesinos* is in direct correlation to our treatment of Jesus. He tells us, "Truly I tell you, just as you did it to one of the least of these who are members of my family, you did it to me."[21] Yet, they are treated as an invisible population by their host communities and churches.

If deliberate and tangible efforts to minister to the *Campesinos* are not established, the church fails in its mission in the following ways:

- Failure to share the love of God with this vulnerable community.
- Failure to listen to their joys and concerns.
- Failure to help them grow spiritually.
- Failure to be blessed by hearing their stories, witnessing their sheer tenacity to provide for their family, and celebrating their faith in God.

On the other hand, a successful ministry will result in a thriving new renewal movement where the *Campesinos* could grow and flourish as they share their gifts and talents with the church. This new renewal movement has the potential to manifest their spiritual "home away from home" where they can fully participate in the worship services. This ministry could also lessen any anxiety they might feel about returning to the farms in future years. The *Campesinos* are a gift to the church and the farming community. They are more than invisible laborers. They are human beings of sacred worth created in the image of God. These people are no different than persons that sit on Sunday mornings at our local

---

20. Matt 25:35–36.
21. Matt 25:40.

houses of worship. As Christians, we must incarnate the love of God to the strangers amongst us. We are called to embrace them as our brothers and sisters. As Methodists, it is part of our Wesleyan DNA.

ASSUMPTIONS

My study assumes that *Campesinos* genuinely desire spiritual care and guidance. This ministry was born from several conversations I had with many of the workers in the blueberry farms of Holland, Michigan. *Campesinos* expressed their desire to be prayed for. They are craving for the word of God through Scripture reading, and they have a hunger to hear the word of God expounded in a relevant sermon. Some also expressed a sincere desire to attend church and enjoy fellowship with other believers.

BIASES

I must disclose my biases in this research. I am an ordained United Methodist deacon in the Rio Texas Conference located in South-Central Texas. My calling from Christ to ministry is rooted both in my *Campesino* heritage and in my United Methodist Hispanic church family. My ministerial role as a deacon is to bring the church into the world—and the world into the church. Deacons are charged to bridge the gap between the church and the world. The work of the deacon includes caring for and ministering to those on the margins and with the help of the Holy Spirit engendering a renewal of the church.

> It is the deacons, in both person and function, whose distinctive ministry is to embody, articulate, and lead the whole people of God in its servant ministry. From the earliest days of the church, deacons were called and set apart for the ministry of love, justice, and service; of

connecting the church with the most needy, neglected, and marginalized among the children of God.[22]

All too often the common perception of *Campesinos* or "migrants" is politically charged and polarizing. Theologically, we understand that poverty is an economic condition, not a comment on a person's value. We read in the Beatitudes, "Blessed are the poor in spirit, for theirs is the kingdom of God."[23] We must affirm our belief that *Campesinos* are loved by God. They have dreams, ambitions, and talents to share with their community and beyond. *Campesinos* often must negotiate their existence in a strange land, conduct business in a foreign language, and live in meager accommodations until the season of seed and harvest ends. "In 2019–2020, two-thirds of farmworkers said that Spanish was the language in which they were most comfortable conversing."[24] In this ever-moving pilgrimage of the *piscas*, our goal is to help them discover that Christ is walking next to them in the crop rows and drinking with them from the irrigation ditches. *Campesinos* have the unique vantage to experience what the Jewish philosopher, Martin Buber called the "I-Thou" relationship with God. Without the façade of materialism, their poverty leaves them only with the confrontations and contemplations of life and death from dawn to dusk; there is nothing to impede a relationship with God. The concept "I-Thou" is best understood as having an intimate, personal relationship with God. The idea of an "I-Thou" connection may also be extended between human beings. There is something divine that occurs in the space of dialogue with another human that facilitates our moving away from an "I-It" association to an "I-Thou" fellowship. Following Buber's analogy, the "I" represents the church and the "Thou" represents the *Campesinos*. It is my hope that the United Methodist Church, with all her bumps and bruises, yet has depths of beauty to be revealed in her outreach to the *Campesinos*.

22. United Methodist Church, *Book of Discipline*, sec. 5, "The Ordained Deacon in Full Connection," para. 319.
23. Matt 5:3.
24. "Findings from the National Agricultural Workers Survey," 13.

La Mesa Campesina

SUMMARY

I was saved and filled with the Holy Spirit when I was thirteen years of age. It was at that tender age when I was mentored by Henry Cleophas "H. C." Ball and his wife, Sunshine Ball. H. C. Ball was licensed as a Methodist and later became a leading pioneer of Hispanic Pentecostalism. Ball was ordained by the Assemblies of God and served them for seventy-four years.[25] In the summer of my thirteenth year, I, along with a Latin American Bible Institute college student, worked with H. C. and Sunshine in a small Hispanic-serving mission church in San Antonio, Texas. Following the Wesleyan tradition, we would rise each morning at 5:00 a.m. for our 6:00 a.m. worship service. H. C., the LABI student, and I would take turns leading the service and preaching. Sunshine was our pianist and vocalist. Looking back, I realize that I always sensed a calling on my life. That is why I pursued ordination. However, I never realized I would come back to my *Campesino* roots.

Although I was raised in an Assemblies of God church, I began my journey back to the United Methodist Church tradition that I had attended as a young child in Crystal City, Texas. As an adult, I attended Drew University, which is affiliated with the United Methodist Church. I was introduced to the theology of John and Charles Wesley by my professor Rev. Dr. Charles "Chuck" Yrigoyen. Dr. Yrigoyen assigned to his class the reading of all the published sermons of John and Charles Wesley. Also, Dr. James Pain, dean of the Casperson School of Graduate Studies at Drew University, introduced me to William Langland's *Piers Plowman*. This fourteenth-century poem speaks about agricultural workers plowing the land as their perceived religious duty. I never thought of bringing Wesley and Langland together for *Campesinos*. My time and studies at Drew brought me back to the United Methodist Church and its tradition of personal and social holiness as described in Scripture.

> You shall love the Lord your God with all your heart, and with all your soul, and with all your mind. This is the

---

25. Rosdahl, "Whatever the Cost," 7.

greatest and first commandment. And a second is like it: "You shall love your neighbor as yourself."[26]

My graduate studies at Yale University Divinity School provided another place for me to explore biblical foundations under my mentor, Dr. Leander Keck. Dr. Lamin Sanneh opened my eyes and heart to mission studies and the importance of translating the message into the vernacular. Finally, two years of living in and assisting at the Charles Wesley house in Bristol, England, gave me insight into the ethos of the Wesleys, the transformative power of the gospel, and the Wesleyan "works of piety" and "works of mercy." Working alongside Aspire Ministry, a homeless ministry housed next to Charles Wesley's House, was truly a "hands-on" approach to ministry. I saw human dignity restored and hearts changed by faith-based mentorship. I am bringing what I learned about the Bible, the Wesleyan tradition, *Piers Plowman*, Archbishop Óscar Romero, Tomás Rivera, and César Chávez to this study. These experiences and learnings uniquely equip me for working with the *Campesinos*.

Campesino ministry was never an intentional act on my part. In fact, it was not until my husband, Daniel Flores, and I moved to Michigan that things started to move in that direction. An invitation from the Michigan Migrant Resource Council was extended to us to attend a festival for the *Campesinos*. At that event, we had the opportunity to visit with some staff members and *Campesinos* in a labor camp. The staff asked if we would like to join them in reaching out to these workers and families. We were also invited to join the Migrant Resource Council monthly meetings. The Council knew that we were clergy, so they allowed us to reach out and visit with the workers. Amazingly, they are the ones who opened the doors for this ministry. As I began to have conversations with the *Campesinos* I felt particularly drawn to them. They were Hispanic, like me. Their struggles were the same struggles my family had experienced when they traveled to work in the fields in other states. How could I not want to help them? How could I not have

---

26. Matt 22:37–39.

compassion for them? How could I not want to share the love of God and the light of his word with them?

My goal is to develop an educational program that will enable churches to understand the plight of the *Campesinos*. I want to help them see that we are all very much the same. We are all individuals struggling with *la vida cotidiana*. That is, we struggle with the messiness of everyday life. We all need Jesus and our faith to help make sense of everything. Hopefully, our understanding will rise beyond cognition to a genuine heart-centered love and concern for these laborers. That would be true renewal. This, however, is only possible through a stirring of the Holy Spirit, prayer, and a genuine desire to serve God and his people.

To recap, my ministry focus is on Hispanic migrant and seasonal agricultural workers in the United States of America. The problem that I am addressing is the lack of spiritual support for the *Campesinos* that are journeying to the *piscas* from their home state of Texas to a northern state such as Michigan. In my next chapter, I will outline the biblical and theological foundations for a practical *Campesino* theology.

Chapter 2

Towards a *Campesino* Theology

THE FOCUS OF THIS CHAPTER will be the thoughtful consideration of biblical and theological resources for ministry with the *Campesinos*. The goal is to develop a practical *Campesino* theology. For biblical expression, I will draw from the Old and New Testaments. The theological resources will reflect the Wesleyan Methodist tradition. They all lend themselves to an appreciation of the value, necessity, and responsibility of reaching the community of migrant agricultural farmworkers.

I. BIBLICAL FOUNDATIONS

A. Moses

The account of the biblical Moses is helpful in the clarification of the *Campesinos'* struggle for liberation. "By faith Moses, when he had grown up, refused to be called the son of pharaoh's daughter, choosing rather to endure ill-treatment with the people of God."[1] Moses, as a member of pharaoh's household, had at his disposal all the wealth, respect, and status that he could ever want. Why would Moses ever want to give up this lifestyle, this life of luxury? I do not believe Moses's decision to turn his back on pharaoh's household

---

1. Heb 11:24–25.

was an impetuous decision. On the contrary, Moses embraced the God of his ancestors and aligned himself with the Israelites as he witnessed their faith modeled amid their struggles. These men and women trusted in God despite their miseries and troubles. Scripture tells us that Moses "considered abuse suffered for the Christ to be greater wealth than the treasures of Egypt, for he was looking ahead to the reward. By faith he left Egypt, unafraid of the king's anger; for he persevered as though he saw him who is invisible."[2]

Moses could have kept himself separate from the oppression and slavery that the Israelites were experiencing. He could have turned his back on his ancestors and continued living with relative ease and comfort. Instead, he chose to share in the struggles of his people.

Campesinos also find themselves in a type of oppression and slavery. The subsistence labor offered through the *piscas* is just enough to keep a vast number of Hispanics living below the poverty line. The *Campesinos* embody this group of Hispanics that are for the most part devalued by the whole of society because of their lack of education, poverty, and inadequate housing.[3] Some churches have paralleled Moses's embracing of his people with their identification with *Campesinos* and their outreach efforts. I was fortunate enough to experience an outpouring of support from area churches. Several Pentecostal and United Methodist churches in Holland and throughout the states of Michigan and Texas became partners in ministry. Through their compassion and empathy, they were compelled to provide non-perishable food items, water, winter jackets, hats, face masks, pillows, blankets, socks, hygiene kits, and monetary donations. I purchased items that were needed and delivered them to the labor camps. And yes, all the items were well received and much appreciated by the *Campesinos*. However good and needed the donations may be, there is no substitute for embracing the people and entering their plight. Moses came to the realization that he could no longer turn a blind eye toward his people and their suffering. He joined them,

2. Heb 11:26–27.
3. González, *Santa Biblia*, 29.

stood with them, and defended the Israelites against the copious injustices they were experiencing at the hands of the Egyptians. It would be well for local churches to follow the precept of identification as demonstrated by Moses. We need to invest ourselves in the lives of these *Campesinos*. We need to actively engage with them to learn about their spiritual yearnings. We need to discover what it is that they crave and long for when it comes to the things of God. The answer to this question can be reached when the local church, like Moses, accepts the people as their own. The church may begin to embrace the *Campesinos* by engaging them in conversation. However, this can only be done if the church takes the initiative to meet them where they are. It is only through intentional interaction and conversations that the church can learn about the struggles, dreams, and spiritual hardships of the *Campesinos*.

B. Amos

In the Old Testament, the prophet Amos provides a biblical model of God's care for rural people. Amos is an example of an agricultural worker used and elevated by God. According to the biblical book that carries his name, Amos, the prophet from Tekoa, earned his living as a livestock breeder and a dresser of sycamore trees.[4] Tekoa was a small town in Judah. It was located south of Jerusalem close to Bethlehem. The Hebrew name Tekoa means "trumpet." A trumpet is not meant to be silent. A trumpet is designed to sound an alarm. God, however, did not select a clergyperson for the important task of conveying his message to his people. Instead, God summoned Amos, a layperson, to sound the alarm to the Israelites. This is significant because any of us can be used by God if we are willing to answer his call. Amos responded in the affirmative and traveled from his home in the southern kingdom of Judah to the northern kingdom of Israel to deliver God's message of justice.

The book of Amos is replete with themes of work, judgment, injustice, sin, and repentance. But this prophetic book further

---

4. Amos 1:1; 7:14.

informs us that God holds his people accountable for the ill-treatment of others. While the Israelites were experiencing a time of financial prosperity and success, they were at the same time plummeting into moral decay, and opportunities to do justice were not on their radar. In chapter 5, verse 24 Amos pleads with the Israelites for justice to roll down like waters and righteousness like an ever-flowing stream. Amos questioned why the wheat prices for the poor were different than the wheat prices for the rich. Why was a bushel of grain from the poor weighed on a different scale than a bushel of grain for the rich?

> Hear this, you that trample on the needy, and bring to ruin the poor of the land, saying, "When will the new moon be over so that we may sell grain; and the Sabbath; so that we may offer wheat for sale?
> We will make the ephah small and the shekel great, and practice deceit with false balances, buying the poor for silver and the needy for a pair of sandals, and selling the sweepings of the wheat."[5]

Amos was an advocate of justice who also spoke out against the mistreatment of the poor. Throughout the text, Amos voices prophetic rage against the injustices of the day. He reminds all of us that faithfulness to God requires more than beautiful worship and fervent prayer. A faithful life is a just and righteous life. Amos proclaims, "But let justice roll down like waters, and righteousness like an ever-flowing stream."[6] God loves the poor and wants his people to demonstrate a compassionate and sympathetic heart toward them. Justice and righteousness begin at an individual level and work outward through the church influencing society until we become an everlasting, always flowing, never-drying-up stream of social justice for the vulnerable and underprivileged in our society: widows, orphans, immigrants, the poor, and the *Campesinos*.

As Christians, it is not good enough to just "do church" by fulfilling our religious practices of singing hymns, raising hands, and praying aloud to God. True worship is validated by treating

---

5. Amos 8:4–6.
6. Amos 5:24.

everyone fairly, and showing mercy, empathy, and love to the vulnerable; in this case, the *Campesinos*. The church needs to begin by acknowledging the presence of *Campesinos* in our society and celebrating their worth.

In the following biblical models, I will offer *Campesino* perspectives on those Scriptures.

C. Ruth

First, I propose that the book of Ruth contains a message about *Campesinos recién llegados,* or newly arrived *Campesinos*. Ruth is about farming folks trying to make a living from the land. They are people of the earth. Naomi and her husband, Elimelech, were forced to leave their home in Bethlehem and move to Moab because of crop failure. Later, Ruth married one of Naomi's sons. She was a Moabite woman born into another place and another faith, but her heart found God. When Ruth's husband died, she followed her mother-in-law to Bethlehem, a village that in Hebrew means "house of bread." Naomi had heard that the fields in Bethlehem were once again fertile and producing an abundance of barley and wheat. These unescorted, highly driven, and determined women were resolved to take a great risk in the hope that it might improve their living situation. Yes, the passage would be treacherous. But staying in Moab was not a viable option.

> The journey from Moab to Judah was extremely dangerous for women. Ten days of journey by foot. The ancient people thought of the desert as a place of evil spirits. It was certainly a place of criminals, wild animals, sparse resources of food, bad water, and unforgiving heat.[7]

Naomi and Ruth can well be regarded as migrant agricultural farmworkers because they traveled from one locale to another. In fact, Bethlehem, in Judah, lies to the north of Moab. Thus, like many of today's *Campesinos*, Naomi and Ruth traveled to *el Norte*. Scripture informs us, "They arrived at the beginning of the barley

7. Flores, "Faith without Walls."

harvest."⁸ Therefore, Ruth immediately began to pick the gleanings from the field. Like *Campesinos* of today, they followed the crops. By doing so God's grace was made manifest through hope when Ruth was able to glean and gather from the corners of Boaz's fields. Ruth and Naomi no longer had to worry about being hungry and destitute.

> This poignant story of faith, love, and redemption pivots on the beauty of the Jewish law that favors the lowly and the oppressed, the widows and the poor. In the Levitical law of gleaning, farmers leave a portion for the poor. This is one of the great portraits of God's grace in the Hebrew Bible. What began as a tragedy reveals itself as a moving example of God's steadfast love.⁹

Gleaning is a form of charity familiar to the Israelites. It is described in several places in the Bible, including Lev 19:9 and 23:22. This Levitical rule is so important it is repeated in Deut 24:19–22. Gleaning permits the poor to gather any grain that is left behind by the harvesters.

> When you reap your harvest in your field and forget a sheaf in the field, you shall not go back to get it; it shall be left for the alien, the orphan, and the widow, so that the Lord your God may bless you in all your undertakings. When you beat your olive trees, do not strip what is left; it shall be for the alien, the orphan, and the widow. When you gather the grapes of your vineyard, do not glean what is left; it shall be for the alien, the orphan, and the widow. Remember that you were a slave in the land of Egypt; therefore, I am commanding you to do this.¹⁰

This ancient practice of welfare allows unharvested crops to be reserved and collected by the needy. Today there are many ways for individuals to take the principle of gleaning and apply it to helping those in need, especially the *Campesinos*. I recently shared a video entitled *The Harvest* [*La Cosecha*] with a Wednesday night

---

8. Ruth 1:22.
9. Flores, "Faith without Walls," 2021.
10. Deut 24:19–22.

Bible study group.[11] It was with this same group that I did a series of lessons on the *Campesinos*. In this video, one of the vignettes is about a young man named Victor. He and his family are *Campesinos*. After a long day of working the *piscas* where Victor and his family harvested tomatoes from sunup to sundown, their pay rate was a paltry $1 for every twenty-five-pound bucket of tomatoes. When the family went to a grocery store to purchase their food supplies for the week, they lamented the fact that even though they harvest tomatoes for a living they were yet unable to purchase this fruit for their own meals. The tomatoes at the store were being sold for $1.99 for a single pound. The family had no choice but to leave empty-handed.

In the story of Ruth, Boaz becomes Ruth's kinsman-redeemer. Boaz is an exquisite illustration of Jesus Christ, who is the kinsman-redeemer for the entire human race. So, what does the Lord require of us? I believe simple acts of reaching out to help others in need are our Christian duty. This is how we care for our neighbors. Why is it that farmers today cannot provide the *Campesinos* with at least some of the produce they harvest for them along with their monetary wages? Wouldn't it have been nice, in the case of Victor's family, if someone at the grocery store had offered to purchase that pound of tomatoes for them?

D. Esther

The book of Esther, also known as the scroll of Esther, is located within the Old Testament. This book does not mention God directly. However, the biblical principles of advocacy are central to the story. The heroes of this story are Esther and Mordecai. Esther was a Jewish girl residing during the time of the diaspora within the Persian Empire. Mordecai was Esther's cousin, but he adopted her as his own daughter upon the death of her parents. Living outside of their homeland signals that it was a time of personal struggle.

---

11. Romano, *Harvest*.

They were living under foreign rule, away from the promised land, and away from the temple.

I propose that the story and message of Esther for the *Campesinos* is one of advocacy. We are not certain how long Esther had been living in exile in Persia; perhaps she was part of the second or third generation. However, we do know that she was able to get into a position that allowed her to be an advocate for her people. Part of this is because she had the skills of diplomacy, biculturalism, and probably bilingualism. In other words, she had the ability to talk with her relative Mordecai, with King Ahasuerus, and with her people, her fellow Jews. It was with that form of advocacy that she was able to turn the heart of the king to save her people.

In our context people who have the skills of biculturalism, the ability to speak and understand more than one language, and the ease and competence of being diplomatic can serve as advocates for the *Campesinos*. Within Hispanic or Latino families, it is not uncommon for second- or third-generation children to serve as the go-betweens. The migrant agricultural children serve as translators during parent–teacher conferences, at hospitals, and doctor's office visits. The children are placed in difficult and often unwanted roles of negotiators in a variety of daily life situations. These minors have the power to change legal decisions because they become the interlocutors between the immigrant and the host. We must acknowledge that one does not need to be Latino to be an advocate for the *Campesinos*. Even though in Esther's case she shared her identity with the people, *Campesinos* simply need people who are willing to serve as allies. In the case of King Ahasuerus, he was not Jewish, yet he was able to be an ally to the Jewish people. Esther provides an example of what we should strive for: piety, faith, courage, caution, and a resolve to help others. Esther serves to inspire all who need help and hope like the poor, the orphan, the widow, and the *Campesinos*.

In the case of Esther as well as with the *Campesinos*, generations pass, and many forget what it is like to be a stranger in a strange land. Many people choose to marry into the dominant culture. Of course, with this comes many opportunities. For example, they learn the language with enough proficiency to go to college and break out of the cycle of traveling to the *piscas*. Former *Campesinos* can pursue and realize their dreams. This is spectacular! However, it risks the throwing away or rejecting of their own culture. Whether this is an intentional act because they are embarrassed by their roots, I cannot say. What I can say is that the book of Leviticus warns us about turning our back on our heritage, on our lineage.

> When an alien resides with you in your land, you shall not oppress the alien. The alien who resides with you shall be to you as the citizen among you; you shall love the alien as yourself, for you were aliens in the land of Egypt: I am The Lord your God.[12]

In the story of Esther, she was part of the Jewish lineage. Esther was an alien in a foreign land. Yet, she became a bridge, an advocate to save her own people. Albeit, Mordecai had to convince Esther to go before King Ahasuerus even if it resulted in a great personal risk to herself. In the following passage, we read Mordecai's persuasive argument reminding Esther of her familial roots and her obligation to her ancestors.

> Do not think that in the king's palace you will escape any more than all the other Jews. For if you keep silence at such a time as this, relief and deliverance will rise for the Jews from another quarter, but you and your father's family will perish. Who knows? Perhaps you have come to royal dignity for just such a time as this.[13]

After several generations of being gone from their homeland, their people, their culture, and their language many people need to be reminded that they were also immigrants. Mordecai's message wasn't just for Esther, it is also applicable to the *Campesinos*. So many of the agricultural farmworkers want to flee and never return to the hard, backbreaking work of the *piscas*. They want to

12. Lev 19:33–34.
13. Esth 4:13b–14.

leave that world far behind. Who can blame them? Many *Campesinos*, especially the youth in their middle to late teenage years, will meet someone in the towns where they are working the harvest and marry them to escape a lifestyle in which they see no future. There they will remain and never return to their homeland. I have an aunt who at the age of sixteen did this very thing. She told me it was the only way she could get out of working in the fields and not be associated with that type of person. It is good to become successful, but it is even better to rise up and be an advocate for someone, especially your own people.

The following is a quote from a German pastor, Martin Niemöller. The words are well known and powerful and they speak of a responsibility that we all share.

> First, they came for the socialists, and I did not speak out—because I was not a socialist.
> Then they came for the trade unionists, and I did not speak out—because I was not a trade unionist.
> Then they came for the Jews, and I did not speak out—because I was not a Jew.
> Then they came for me—and there was no one left to speak for me.[14]

As Christians, when opportunities arise to serve God and our neighbor, we should each consider why God has allowed us to be in certain places. Let us use our God-given gifts and graces to bolster and encourage the poor, the widow, the orphan, and the *Campesinos* by advocating for them.

E. Jesus

In the Gospels, Jesus often used agricultural metaphors in his teachings to rural people. These stories were meant to stimulate the imagination while at the same time bringing to question the

---

14. "Despite diligent search, the original occasion on which this saying was used, and its original form, cannot yet be established. Niemöller used it in various wordings and on numerous occasions." Conway, "Political Theology of Martin Niemöller," 540.

customary values of the time. Jesus knew his audience. They were farmers and very familiar with what farm work required. They understood that crops needed to be planted, fertilized, watered, and protected against hail, hard freezes, animals, and scorching droughts. When the fruits and vegetables were ripe, they had to be harvested. Each day rain or shine, hot or cold, the *Campesinos* go out to toil in the fields. This is not just the work of their hands, for many it is their identity and heritage. The agricultural language and metaphors were something that they were accustomed to hearing, and they could easily comprehend Jesus's words and respond to him.

Jesus utilized the agrarian vernacular as opposed to the theological jargon of the rabbis to demonstrate the importance of speaking in a language the people were familiar with and could easily understand. Jesus moved seamlessly into their world by speaking their heart language. Jesus's action conveyed not only his love for the *Campesinos* but his appreciation and acceptance of them, their idioms, and their culture. This simple yet significant and intentional act translated into a testament to God's care and tenderness for the *Campesinos*. It is from Jesus that we receive the mandate and the example of how to care for the poor and the oppressed in our communities.

Jesus used scenes from everyday life to illustrate his points about the gospel and the kingdom of God. For example, take the parable of the good tree and the bad tree.

> Every good tree bears good fruit, but the bad tree bears bad fruit. A good tree cannot bear bad fruit, nor can a bad tree bear good fruit.[15]

The *Campesino* being familiar with various fruit trees such as apple, cherry, and peach would easily be able to identify a good tree from a bad tree. They would also be able to comprehend Jesus's message that what is inside a person is what will be produced as fruit, either wholesome or corrupt. Everything in nature produces after its own kind. Therefore, Jesus's concern lies both with the quality of the

15. Matt 7:17–18.

fruit and with the tree itself. A *Campesino* would know better than to harvest and accept any fruit from a diseased and/or a decaying tree. Their training and intuition enable them to assess the situation when a stranger, be it a clergyperson or a layperson, comes to visit them. The *Campesinos* are searching to see if the fruits and the tree, i.e., the missioners, are good or bad. It is for this reason that the laborers initially seem reticent to engage in conversation. They have learned it is necessary to protect themselves from would-be offenders.

The following parable about the sower can be found in both the Gospel of Luke and the Gospel of Matthew.

> Listen! A sower went out to sow. And as he sowed, some seeds fell on the path, and the birds came and ate them up. Other seeds fell on rocky ground, where they did not have much soil, and they sprang up quickly, since they had no depth of soil. But when the sun rose, they were scorched; and since they had no root, they withered away.[16]

This teaching would not be lost on the *Campesinos*. The sower represents God, and the seed is his message. As the workers are accustomed to having their hands in the soil and tending to all kinds of vegetation, the *Campesinos* are familiar with plant development. By examining the root structure, the laborers understand the correlation between the viability of a plant and its roots.

In the Gospel of John, Jesus told a story about a grain of wheat.

> Consider a grain of wheat. Very truly, I will tell you, unless a grain of wheat falls into the earth and dies, it remains just a single grain; but if it dies, it bears much fruit.[17]

The parable of the grain of wheat would be easily grasped by the agricultural laborers. By necessity, a seed must be planted in nutrient-rich soil to become what it was always meant to be. Jesus

16. Luke 8:5; Matt 13:3.
17. John 12:24.

tells us that if the grain does not die, it will remain just a single, solitary grain. However, if it yields itself, that one grain of wheat produces five or more heads with over twenty-two grains each.[18] By this calculation one grain of wheat can produce at least three hundred and twenty grains of wheat. Of course, it all hinges on whether that individual grain of wheat or person is willing to give him/herself completely to fulfill their ultimate purpose in Christ. That is, spreading the story of the good news of salvation to everyone, including the *Campesinos*.

In the Gospel of Mark, we learn that God's kingdom among us also begins as a seed—something small and outwardly insignificant. But inside of it, there is greatness.

> With what can we compare the kingdom of God, or what parable will we use for it? It is like a mustard seed, which, when sown upon the ground, is the smallest of all the seeds on earth; yet when it is sown it grows up and becomes the greatest of all shrubs, and puts forth large branches, so that the birds of the air can make nests in the shade.[19]

We can compare the *Campesinos* to the mustard seed. At first glance, they appear small and insignificant. But with a little faith, a kind word, a smile, a thoughtful gesture, a listening ear, soon the seed of the gospel of Jesus Christ will take, sprout, and begin to grow within them. Only God knows how large of an impact the *Campesinos* could have on the church at large.

The Gospel of Mark provides us with further instruction on farmers and the *Campesinos*. For example, this parable of the sprouting seed suggests a potential harvest.

> The kingdom of God is as if someone would scatter seed on the ground. And would sleep and rise night and day, and the seed would sprout and grow, he does not know how. The earth produces of itself, first the stalk, then the head, then the full grain in the head. But when the grain

18. Lyon and Klein, "Estimating Winter Wheat Grain Yields."
19. Mark 4:30–32.

is ripe, at once he goes in with his sickle, because the harvest has come.[20]

The harvest that Jesus spoke about is a call to go and evangelize, teaching the word of God and sharing his love with others through works of mercy. The harvest could produce the fruits of charity and justice that come through God's grace. Jesus informs us, "The harvest is abundant, but the laborers are few; so, ask the master of the harvest to send out laborers for his harvest."[21] This type of speech is familiar to the *Campesinos*. They know what it is to be sent into the field. What Jesus is saying to us is that there are so few willing to minister to the poor and the oppressed. We need to be the hands and feet of Christ planting his word in the hearts of the *Campesinos*, following the biblical example checking on them night and day, and nurturing them until they are fully mature in God's love.

F. James

James, the brother of Jesus, speaks to the church and the farmer about how to ethically treat the poor, the *Campesinos*. In the first six verses of chapter 5 James is delivering a warning to the rich oppressors.

> Come now, you rich people, weep and wail for the miseries that are coming to you. Your riches have rotted, and your clothes are moth-eaten. Your gold and silver have rusted, and their rust will be evidence against you, and it will eat your flesh like fire. You have laid up treasure for the last days. Listen! The wages of the laborers who mowed your fields, which you kept back by fraud, cry out, and the cries of the harvesters have reached the ears of the Lord of hosts. You have lived on the earth in luxury and in pleasure; you have fattened your hearts in a day of

---

20. Mark 4:26–29.
21. Matt 9:37.

slaughter. You have condemned and murdered the righteous one, who does not resist you.²²

This is the prophetic voice seeking justice for the *Campesinos*. James tells the rich landowners, "You will not get away with oppressing the laborers, the ones who have done your reaping." God loves the poor and the oppressed and he has heard their cries. The cries of the *Campesinos* have reached the ears of the Lord of hosts. James condemns those who would rather amass their wealth than show mercy and justice to the *Campesinos*.

This type of abusive treatment was also evidenced in the lives of the migrant agricultural workers of Crystal City, Texas. These *Campesinos* were treated horrifically. The housing that was provided for them during the 1930s and early 1940s also doubled as a prison for the undocumented aliens who had been arrested for border violations. So, the housing was a combination of labor camp and prison. The labor camp was comprised of:

> 41 cottages and 118 one-room shelters, none had running water. The workers were forced to use outdoor privies. They slept on cots and hung their work clothes on nails. . . . When Mexican laborers at the camp failed to produce, some ranchers resorted to locking them in tiny chicken coops. Mexicans were viewed by Anglos as a subservient class, cogs in the wheels of business and daily life.²³

The maltreatment of the *Campesinos* throughout the United States has historically been racially biased and fueled by greed. It is worthy to hear the words of James once again as he sounds the alarm and tells the rich oppressor, "You have lived on the earth in luxury and in pleasure; you have fattened your hearts in a day of slaughter. You have condemned and murdered the righteous one, who does not resist you."²⁴ Christians are admonished to align themselves with and join their collective voices together

---

22. Jas 5:1–6.
23. Russell, *Train to Crystal City*, 43.
24. Jas 5:5–6.

with James's and sound the alarm to end the mistreatment of the *Campesinos* and give them the hope of God's love.

II. THEOLOGICAL FOUNDATIONS

A. John Wesley

As a United Methodist clergyperson, I first look to the teachings and precepts of the Bible, but I also look for insights and examples that our founder, John Wesley, might provide. In John Wesley's Sermon 92 "On Zeal," he exhorts his listeners that when someone is in need, helping that person takes precedence over prayer and other works of piety.[25] Wesley was a man of prayer, Scripture reading, and worship, but he had an even greater zeal for works of mercy. Works of mercy include doing good works, feeding the hungry, clothing the naked, visiting the sick and the imprisoned, seeking justice, and finding an end to oppression and discrimination. I interpret this as a personal call to minister to the *Campesinos*.

In John Wesley's formative years, he learned the value of hard work and the struggles that came with poverty. His father, Samuel Wesley, was an Anglican priest and he had one of the lowest-paying parishes in England. Samuel and Susanna, John's mother, had nineteen children, but only ten survived infancy. This was quite a large family to support and feed so all the children had to help and do their part. The Wesley family was well acquainted with poverty and debt and John had witnessed his own father carted off to debtor's prison. While Samuel was in prison, Susanna took care of the household and children but was compelled to offer Bible studies in her kitchen to any who would attend. It is no wonder with such an upbringing, John would feel compelled to help feed the hungry, clothe the naked, and care for their souls as well.

Ministry with the *Campesinos* by necessity involves works of mercy. In my efforts to reach the *Campesinos,* I realized the work was too immense to do on my own. So, I partnered with various state and county agencies as well as church and parachurch

25. Wesley, *Works*, 314.

organizations across the State of Michigan to help meet some of the physical needs of the laborers. Parachurch organizations are Christian faith-based organizations that work across denominations to help with things that churches may not be able to do on their own. Although my focus is on meeting the spiritual needs of the *Campesinos*, I am keenly aware that sometimes it is more important to follow John Wesley's teaching and first fulfill the physical necessities of food and clothing. By doing so, we express God's love in tangible ways while at the same time we are building trust between ourselves and the *Campesinos*.

I cannot emphasize enough the importance of building trust within this community. They have learned to be cautious in their dealings with people outside of their immediate connections because they have too often been mistreated. However, I learned that with repeated visits and interactions this community of laborers kindly received and welcomed me as one of their own. We reached a point in the relationship that changed from transactional to familiarity and trust. They were no longer afraid, or suspicious, nor timid and shy. They began to share the needs of their heart with me and the ministry team with me. Trust had taken root. This is the point at which ministry naturally transitioned into spiritual matters.

B. Justo González

Justo González is a Cuban American theologian and an ordained United Methodist elder. He is a retired member of the former Rio Grande Conference, a historically Hispanic-serving conference. The Rio Grande Conference merged in 2015 with the Southwest Texas Conference, a predominately Anglo conference. The new conference is now known as the Rio Texas Conference of the United Methodist Church. González is a leading voice in the field of Hispanic theology, having written more than two dozen books. In his book entitled, *¡Alabadle! Hispanic Christian Worship*, published in 1996, González discusses from a Hispanic perspective what it is like to enter a dominant culture's worship experience.

La Mesa Campesina

> There is probably no place where the feeling of exile and alienness becomes more poignant for me than when I attend worship in most Anglo churches. . . . I am among sisters and brothers in Christ. I believe what they believe. . . . Most of them are friendly and loving people who have every intention of making me feel included and at home. I am in church, the spiritual home for the homeless. . . . And yet, I am not at home. . . . Even in the midst of worship, I find myself athirst, "as a deer longing for flowing streams."[26]

González goes on to say that this is a painful experience for the visiting worshiper. But it would be equally painful if the church people knew what their visitors were experiencing. Therefore, instead of fully entering and participating in the corporate act of worship, the Hispanic worshiper alternatively enters into a time of private devotion.

Perhaps, one way we can begin to appreciate one another is if we were to follow Justo Gonzalez's suggestion of reading the Bible through Hispanic eyes. But how can non-Hispanics do this? I would suggest that we read the Bible with empathy toward Hispanics. That is, those who preserve their Hispanic identity and read the Bible from the life experiences of the Latino/a struggle to fulfill and excel at what God wants us to be.[27] The struggle that González raises is the struggle for salvation or liberation.[28] I would further challenge the church universal to go one step further and read Holy Scripture through the eyes of the *Campesinos*. The stories, efforts, and position of the *Campesinos* are uniquely theirs and not necessarily part of the general US Latino/a experience. Latino/a *Campesinos* have a myriad of historical and distinct experiences that ought to be highlighted.

We must acknowledge the strength of character and determination of the *Campesinos*. They are more than field workers. They are our brothers and sisters. We may use the analogy of a

---

26. González, *¡Alabadle!*, 17.
27. González, *Santa Biblia*, 29.
28. González, *Santa Biblia*, 29.

fiesta which I call *La Mesa Campesina* to represent a new model of ministry. Consistent with this imagery, the church invites these *Campesinos* to bring their sitting stools or *taburetes* and be part of a vibrant faith community that recognizes them, celebrates their cultural values, and offers spiritual resources that will nurture them. This is a Sabbath time of rest from their labors. They will find at *La Mesa Campesina* a rich *fiesta* that honors their life experiences of pilgrimage, mortality, family, prayer, and the sacraments.

CONCLUSION

In conclusion, from both our Old and New Testaments, we gain confidence and inspiration and a mandate to embrace and defend the poor, the oppressed, and the *Campesino*. The biblical examples arise from the story of Moses and the prophetic voice of Amos. Ruth and Esther bring the female perspective to the table. This is an essential element of *La Mesa Campesina*. They both demonstrate their power, intelligence, determination, and courage. Jesus also demonstrates the importance of speaking in a language or idiom that is recognizable and appreciated. His message conveyed love and compassion to the poor and the oppressed. James's message, like the other biblical examples, speaks in favor of the ethical treatment of the poor and the accountability of the rich. Each story demonstrates the importance of caring for our neighbors and sharing in the struggles of the *Campesinos*. It is time for the church to stand alongside the laborers to defend them against injustices but also to present them with the word of God.

Chapter 3

Reading to Understand *Campesinos*

THERE IS VERY LITTLE written by Protestant Evangelicals about migrant ministry. An exception is *Sowing the Sacred*, an excellent historical analysis of Pentecostal farmworkers in California written by Lloyd Daniel Barba.[1] For that reason, I am drawing from a broad base of spiritual and cultural literature that reflects "God-talk" in rural contexts. My literary sources include William Langland's *Piers Plowman*, the *Shepherd of Hermas*, St. Augustine's *Teaching Christianity*, Tomás Rivera's novel *Y No se lo Tragó la Tierra*, select biographical material about César Chávez, and spiritual writings of Oscar Romero. I will also be drawing from Michael J. Gorman's *Cruciformity: Paul's Narrative Spirituality of the Cross* and Eldin Villafañe's *Beyond Cheap Grace: A Call to Radical Discipleship, Incarnation, and Justice*.

I. WILLIAM LANGLAND'S *PIERS PLOWMAN*

Piers Plowman is a medieval English poem from the fourteenth century written by William Langland. The character, Piers Plowman, serves as Langland's guide in discovering the way to Truth. Langland enlivens our eyes and ears with a presentation of

1. Barba, *Sowing the Sacred*.

Christian history through the medium of several dream visions. These visions propel the reader on his or her journey from beginning to end. Langland's journey is a pilgrimage that will lead him to his "aha" moment. In the prologue of this poem, one can grasp humanity's situation as envisioned by Langland.

> There I dreamed a dream that was indeed wonderful:
> I was in a wilderness, but where I knew not.
> I set my face eastward, where, high against the sun,
> I saw a tower, trim-built on the top of a hill;
> And a deep dale beneath it, and a dungeon in it,
> With deep dark dykes that were dreadful to see.
> A pleasant plain full of people lay between these places,
> With every manner of man, poor, middling, and rich,
> Toiling or traveling as the world's way took them.
> Some spent their lives at the plough, and were seldom idle,
> Seeding and sowing and strongly labouring
> To gather what the gluttony of wastrels would again scatter.
> Some spend their lives in pride, and were dressed in apt style,
> Coming all tricked-out in conspicuous clothing.[2]

The poem begins with Langland wandering the world as a hermit. One day, he lies down by a stream, falls into a deep sleep, and dreams this extraordinary dream. In this dream, he sees a field full of people. They are people from all walks of life, the poor, the rich, and those in between. The field is sandwiched between a beautiful castle on a hill and an ominous-looking dungeon in a valley. Langland watches the people in the field and is astonished. The people are doing what they would normally do to occupy their time—plowing, buying, selling, begging, etc. There is no focus on spiritual matters. They are not aware of the danger that is so perilously situated. Langland noticed that they were totally oblivious to their close proximity to hell. But more importantly, they were inattentive of just how close they were to heaven.

Langland was on a quest to live a good Christian life. Along the way, he meets different characters that will assist him on his journey. One such character is Piers, a humble plowman. He is

---

2. Langland, *Piers Plowman*, Prologue, 3, lines 11–24.

the one who leads the people through a plowing field. He is also the one that knows the way to Truth. Piers represents a model of Christian behavior and good works. Piers offers to help guide the people if they will help him plow his field. He substitutes agricultural labor for the pilgrimage. This poem explicitly connects work with Christian virtue.

Langland believes that hard work, honest living, and charity are what will lead the pilgrim to their encounter with Truth, with God. Piers equates plowing with pilgrimage. Piers is a man of the earth who works hard with his hands and is subjected to harsh weather conditions as he plants his crop. This is evidenced in the following:

> Said Piers, "I shall put on, then, a pilgrim's dress,
> And take you all with me until we find Truth.
> I shall put on my poor clothes, all ragged and patched,
> My gaiters, and my gloves to get warmth in my fingers,
> Sling my seed-bag round my neck instead of a scrip,
> And bring along in it a bushel of bread-corn.
> This I myself will sow, and then soon after
> Will pilgrim-it like a palmer, in search of pardon.[3]

The plowman's description of himself tells us that he is poor. His ragged and patched clothes are his pilgrim's dress. The seed bag is what he carries around his neck instead of a wallet. He continues to describe the work of his hands. He is sowing approximately thirty-two quarts of cereal grain like barley or rye.

This is an important lesson for the *Campesinos*. There should be no shame associated with working in the *piscas*. Whether it involves plowing, sowing, or harvesting there is dignity in this work. Colossians informs us, "Whatever your task, put yourselves into it, as done for the Lord and not for your masters, since you know that from the Lord you will receive the inheritance as your reward; you serve the Lord Christ."[4]

The *Campesinos* need to be reminded that the work of their hands is as a pilgrimage unto the Lord. They can have an encounter

---

3. Langland, *Piers Plowman*, Passus 6, 61, lines 59–66.
4. Col 3:23–24.

with God right there in the blueberry fields, or amid the tomatoes, cucumbers, or onion furrows. Jesus also tells us, "No one who puts the hand to the plow and looks back is fit for the kingdom of God."[5] The message that we must convey to the *Campesinos* and embrace for ourselves is we must not become distracted or diverted from our plowing, our pilgrimage, and our encounter with God. Of course, it would be good if the cyclical nature of working in the *piscas* could be broken. However, in its absence, the church must do all it can to restore dignity to the *Campesinos*.[6] The laborers need to be assured that they too are fulfilling their calling to God. And more importantly, God is with them as they execute their pilgrimage of plowing, sowing, and harvesting. God is made manifest in their lives through their steadfast devotion.

Like farming, this journey or pilgrimage is complicated. For a *Campesino* it may appear that they are experiencing a time of exile. Yes, in a manner of speaking they are forced away from their home. They have left whatever creature comforts their homes may have provided to travel to an unknown location and experience a diaspora, or a scattering of themselves away from their friends and other family members. But this exile, this diaspora, is partly of their own choosing, and they may return home at their own discretion. Like going into exile, a pilgrimage is not a journey that is achieved easily or instantaneously. Physically, the *Campesinos* may find this to be an arduous journey from their home to the farms away from home. They fully understand that this is their way of life. Every year they will go to the camp and return home hopefully with enough money to last them until the following year. This is the nature of the *piscas*. The change of seasons will beckon them to make their pilgrimage once again. This pilgrimage can be filled with anxiety and perhaps fear of not knowing exactly what

---

5. Luke 9:62.

6. Mathews, *Slavery and Methodism*, 78. In the times of American slavery, Methodist missionaries to slaves emphasized scriptures about obedience to their masters. But unlike the Presbyterians and Episcopalians, the Methodists left out statements about the equality of men before God to which masters were also accountable. *In La Mesa Campesina* we are all equally accountable to God including the farmers and the ranchers.

to expect at their destination. Will they be well received, and will their housing be adequate for their family?

Piers Plowman, the character in the story, is teaching William Langland that a pilgrimage is a progression, the soul's progression from being self-serving to loving the Lord God with single-minded devotion. This kind of devotion causes one to yield one's life completely to God and yearn for him with every fiber of one's being. "As a deer longs for flowing streams, so my soul longs for you, O God. My soul thirsts for God, for the living God. When shall I come and behold the face of God?"[7]

Langland's quest for "Truth" began with a realization of good and evil, and heaven and hell. It was at this point that his spiritual eyes were opened. He was forced to examine his life. The church assisted by teaching him about truth and falsehood. Thus, equipped with the basics, he began his pilgrimage. His journey was not a simple one or for that matter a speedy one. A single encounter is not the ultimate goal. We are to renew that relationship daily. We must, by necessity, work out our salvation by loving God with our entire being. Only then, through the merits of God's grace, might we be able to love our neighbor as much as ourselves. Our responsibility to the *Campesinos* does not end with a single encounter. We must journey with them on this pilgrimage to Truth and nurture them as they grow in God's grace.

II. THE SHEPHERD OF HERMAS

Another popular story in the ancient church was the *Shepherd of Hermas*. Philip Schaff says it is the "oldest Christian allegory . . . and it has been compared with Bunyan's *Pilgrim Progress* and Dante's *Commedia*."[8] In the *Shepherd of Hermas,* Hermas, like Piers Plowman, receives instruction through visions. Hermas's visions are from an angel that is dressed like a shepherd. The purpose of

---

7. Ps 42:1–2.
8. Schaff, *History of the Christian Church*, 680.

the angel's message is "to call Hermas and through him the church to repentance."⁹

As a device when writing about the *Shepherd of Hermas*, Schaff utilizes the genre of religious romance. These stories were widely held because they spoke the language of the populace. This is a lesson that must be mastered. Lamin Sanneh, my former Yale professor, often said, "The message must be translated."¹⁰ In other words, we must speak so as to be understood. Hans-Georg Gadamer, in his book, *Truth and Method*, agrees with Sanneh. "No text and no book speaks if it does not speak a language that reaches the other person."¹¹ I am convinced that it is the third person of the Trinity, the Holy Spirit, who illumines our mind so that we might understand the love of God as expressed through his words. The gospel proclamation requires the word's quickening by the Holy Spirit in human hearts.

III. TOMÁS RIVERA'S *Y NO SE LO TRAGÓ LA TIERRA*

My familiarity with *Campesinos* is rooted in the fact that I was born in Crystal City, Texas, a migrant agricultural worker town in South Texas. This is a place where poverty and food insecurity are a way of life. One of the sons of that community was Tomás Rivera. He was one of my father's lifelong friends. Rivera wrote a semi-autobiographical novel, *Y No se lo Tragó la Tierra . . . And the Earth Did Not Devour Him*, about the migrant life of the 1940s and 1950s. He tells the story through the eyes of a young boy from Crystal City. This book resonated with me because my grandparents, parents, and mother-in-law were all *Campesinos*. They understood the harshness of picking cotton in the hot Texas sun. Rivera's family would also travel, like other families, from Crystal City to *el Norte*, the North. They were familiar with what it

9. Schaff, *History of the Christian Church*, 680.
10. Class lecture in World Christianity: Religious and Cultural Issues, 1998.
11. Gadamer, *Truth and Method*, 398.

La Mesa Campesina

was like to travel from South Texas to Michigan, Minnesota, and Wisconsin riding on top of a truck laden with crops while searching for work in the harvest fields. In addition to the long days of uncomfortable travel, these trips to the *piscas* added further stress to their lives by subjecting them to hunger, loneliness, alienation, poverty, and discrimination.

Despite his difficult upbringing, Tomás Rivera was the first Mexican American in Crystal City to earn and receive his doctor of philosophy degree. This was quite an accomplishment considering the limited literacy, high poverty, and outright racism Mexican Americans faced in those days. Rivera demonstrates from a *Campesino*'s perspective the cruel and painful reality of life. Even as a young boy, he understood his life and he hated it. Rivera was one of those rare individuals who was too intelligent, too outspoken, too rebellious, and too much of a thinker. He would analyze a situation and come up with his own conclusion. Not even his mother could persuade him otherwise.

When his father suffered a heat stroke in the fields, Rivera's character shares the feelings of anger and rage that he internalized. The following is a portion of a conversation between him and his mother on the occasion of his father's illness.

> Se hubieran venido luego luego, m'ijo. ¿No veían que su tata estaba enfermo? Ustedes sabían muy bien que estaba picado del sol. ¿Por qué no se vinieron?
>
> Pos, no sé. . . . Yo como quiera sí le dije que se sentara debajo del árbol que está a la orilla de los surcos, pero él no quiso. Fue cuando empezó a vomitar.[12]

> You should've come right away, m'ijo.
> Couldn't you see that your Daddy was sick?
> You should have known that he'd suffered a sunstroke.
> Why didn't you come home?

---

12. Rivera, *Y No se lo Tragó la Tierra*, 32.

> I don't know. . . . But I did tell him to sit down under the tree that's at the end of the rows, but he did not want to. And that is when he started throwing up.[13]

Rivera continues to reveal the depth of anger rooted in their lifestyle of *Campesino* work. The unnamed character in his book witnessed his mother praying, lighting candles, and washing his sick father's scapularies.

> ¿Que se gana, mamá, con andar haciendo eso? ¿A poco cree que le ayudó mucho a mi tío y a mi tía? ¿Por qué es que nosotros estamos aquí como enterrados en la tierra? O los microbios nos comen o el sol nos asolea. Siempre alguna enfermedad . . . Y luego ellos rogándole a Dios . . . si Dios no se acuerda de uno. . . . ¿Por qué nosotros nomas enterrados en la tierra como animales sin ningunas esperanzas de nada? . . . No me diga nada. Ya sé lo que me va a decir – que los pobres van al cielo.[14]

> What is to be gained from doing all that, Mother? Don't tell me you think it helped my aunt and uncle any. How come we're like this, like we're buried alive? Either the germs eat us alive or the sun burns us up. Always some kind of sickness . . . begging for God's help . . . why, God doesn't care about us. . . . Why us, burrowed in the dirt like animals with no hope for anything? . . . Don't say it. I know what you are going to tell me—that the poor go to heaven.[15]

As we read the little boy's words, we can hear his frustration with having to live the life of a *Campesino*. He blamed God for their troubles even when he learned that his father was on the road to recovery. He witnessed a lot of pain and death at a young age and from his experience, he knew that sooner or later death would win. So, in his anger, the boy cried out in a belligerent victory kicking

---

13. Rivera, *Y No se lo Tragó la Tierra*, 108.
14. Rivera, *Y No se lo Tragó la Tierra*, 33, 34.
15. Rivera, *Y No se lo Tragó la Tierra*, 109, 110.

the earth. "Not yet, you can't swallow me up yet."[16] His was a life that seemed hopeless and without any apparent church presence or guidance. Tomás Rivera's family, specifically his mother, depended on folk spirituality and rituals.

Rivera's novel represents a life without hope, a life filled with anger, fear, and insecurity. As Christians, it is our responsibility to offer the *Campesinos* hope and God's grace. Hope is born from our human experience and interrupted by the inspiration of God's presence in our lives. "This hope doesn't put us to shame, because the love of God has been poured out in our hearts through the Holy Spirit, who has been given to us."[17]

I include Rivera's novel because we must acknowledge that we will not always be able to reach everyone with the gospel message. As painful as that reality may be, we should not give up on our outreach. The apostle Paul, tells us, "I planted, Apollos watered, but God gave the growth. So, neither the one who plants nor the one who waters is anything, but only God who gives the growth."[18] We are in no position to save anyone. But it is our mission, our responsibility, and our calling as disciples of Jesus Christ to present and demonstrate the gospel message of Jesus's love to all, including the *Campesinos*.

IV. CÉSAR CHÁVEZ

César Chávez was a Roman Catholic Christian who was influenced by the nonviolence practices and teachings of Gandhi and Martin Luther King Jr. Chávez worked all his life to improve agricultural business practices. Because he experienced firsthand what it was like to work the *piscas* and to be treated less than human, he focused his efforts on improving the treatment of the *Campesinos* and the working conditions out in the fields.

---

16. Rivera, *Y No se lo Tragó la Tierra*, 112.
17. Rom 5:5.
18. 1 Cor 3:6–7.

Reading to Understand Campesinos

To understand his driving force, we need to consider his upbringing. Chávez was brought up in a Mexican form of Roman Catholicism. United Methodists recognize Roman Catholics as our ecumenical partners. For most Mexicans and other Latinas/os, Catholicism is not just their religion, it is who they are. This identity is passed on with great pride through their family as a legacy. This is exactly how César Chávez was nurtured: "His spirituality was shaped by his family and grounded in what Latino/a theologians have termed 'Abuelita Theology.'"[19]

Chávez's family lived away from the city because of segregated housing. Because they lived outside of the city of Yuma, catechism classes were not easily accessible. Therefore, his grandmother taught him the tenets of the Roman Catholic faith.

> Mama Tella [grandmother] gave us our formal religious training.... She was always praying, just praying. Every evening she would sit in bed, and we would gather in front of her.... After the Rosary she would tell us about a particular saint and drill us on our Catechism.[20]

After Chávez's grandmother taught them all she knew, the family traveled to the Catholic parish church in Yuma, Arizona. They went to ask the priest to allow them to complete their first communion. Of course, the priest did not want to give his permission, stating that they must attend the church's catechism classes.

> The Anglo priest refused saying . . . they have not had any religious training. They can't take communion . . . they must attend class here in Yuma first. To this, Juana [mother] retorted, "They can't because we live out in the valley twenty miles away. We can't travel that far every week." She firmly insisted, "Well, ask them something" . . . The priest proceeded to drill the Chávez children with questions from the Catholic catechism, and because of their thorough training in "*abuelita* theology," César

---

19. Romero, *Brown Church*, 124.
20. Garcia, *Gospel of César Chávez*, 26–27.

and Rita [sister] passed with flying colors. The children received their first communion the following day.[21]

Chávez was deeply influenced by his mother's *dichos*, "Abuelita Theology," and his Christian faith. He was first exposed to the notion of nonviolence through his mother, Juana. Her instruction came in the form of *dichos*, or proverbs. Juana did not want her son to grow up thinking that physical violence was the only way to defend himself. For example, "It's best to turn the other cheek," she would say, "God gave you senses like your eyes and mind and tongue so that you can get out of anything."[22]

César Chávez and his family, like Rivera's family, were also *Campesinos*. Working in the *piscas* allowed Chávez to wholly experience the appalling working conditions and the mistreatment of the *Campesinos*. Chávez, unlike Rivera, channeled his anger into creating the National Farm Workers Association. His firsthand knowledge as a *Campesino* and his association with union organizers such as Dolores Huerta and Fred Ross, who were also passionate to right the wrongs done to the Hispanic laborers, led to the development of a movement that is still to this day in operation.[23]

The uniqueness of Chávez's organization was that it was rooted in his Christian faith. He did his work in the name of Jesus. His farmworkers movement was first and foremost a faith-based movement. Chávez successfully and creatively fused Mexican Catholicism with the social justice teachings of Catholicism. He was familiar with and understood the uniting power of *La Virgen de Guadalupe*.

> La Virgen points us to Christ, and she has been a powerful symbol of the fact that God loves the indigenous people of Mexico and is their protector.... Many Latinas and Latinos in the United States look to La Virgen as a symbol of faith, identity, hope, female empowerment, and cultural liberation.[24]

21. Romero, *Brown Church*, 125.
22. Ferriss and Sandoval, *Fight in the Fields*, 13.
23. Dalton, *Moral Vision of César Chávez*, 15.
24. González and González, *Christianity in Latin America*, 56, 58.

La Virgen was the central religious symbol for the National Farm Workers Association. And fellow activist Dolores Huerta honored her as well.

> She is a symbol of the impossible, of doing the impossible to win a victory, in humility, of being able to win with the faith. I mean that's the important thing that she symbolizes to the union: that with faith you can win. You know with faith you can overcome.[25]

César Chávez challenged the injustices against farmworkers by using the Christian faith to unify the farmworkers under the banner of *La Virgen de Guadalupe*. In 1966, he fashioned his famous march from the Central Valley to Sacramento as a penitential pilgrimage or *peregrinacion*. Drawing from popular Mexican religious tradition, he called the march "Penitence, Pilgrimage, and Revolution."[26] Beginning on July 4, 1966, the Texas Farmworkers launched their own march in support of and in the spirit of César Chávez's pilgrimage. Every day the marchers would start with prayer. This 490-mile Texas pilgrimage was an ecumenical endeavor. This peaceful march began in Rio Grande City and zigzagged its way through such southern Texas towns as McAllen, Corpus Christi, Kenedy, San Antonio, and New Braunfels, finally arriving at the state capital in Austin on Labor Day, September 5, 1966.[27] These *Campesinos* were protesting "the 40 cents-an-hour pittance they were being paid."[28] They were hoping to increase the hourly wage to the federal minimum pay of $1.25. *El Buen Samaritano* United Methodist Church located in Kenedy, Texas, under the leadership of Rev. Isabel Gomez, was one of the few Protestant churches that gave respite to the marchers.[29] While most Protestants would not promote the veneration of *La Virgen*, it is important to recognize the potency of the religious and

---

25. Dolores Huerta, quoted in Romero, *Brown Church*, 69.
26. Garcia, *Gospel of César Chávez*, 12, 16.
27. Smith, "1966 Farmworkers' Strike March Route."
28. Ramirez, "Melon Pickers Strike," 4.
29. Gomez, "Remembrances of La Marcha."

cultural symbol for Mexican Catholics. César Chávez understood his Hispanic and Latino/a people well. It was not only the marchers of Delano, California, that carried with them images of *La Virgen de Guadalupe* but also the *Campesinos* of Texas. United Methodist Bishop Joel N. Martinez (ret.) stated at a lecture recently that when he joined the march in Kenedy, "one of the priests thrust into my hands four things to carry: a crucifix, an image of Our Lady of Guadalupe, a U.S. flag, and a Mexican flag."[30]

The inclusion of such terms as "penitence" and "pilgrimage" reveals how much Chávez was influenced by his Catholic faith. Along with these two, fasting and prayer also played a critical role in his leadership. The purpose of joining together prayer with fasting is to connect us with God. Fasting is biblical, and examples can be found within the Old and New Testaments. In Nehemiah 9, the Israelites fasted and lifted prayers of praise and confession after sinning against God. In Esth 4:16, Queen Esther fasts with Israel and prays for the strength and courage to approach King Ahasuerus and ask that Israel might be spared from Haman's plot. In the book of Daniel, chapter 9, we are informed that Daniel is fasting and praying for the people because of their disobedience. He asked God to have mercy on the chosen people. In Matt 4:1–11 Jesus fasts for forty days and forty nights.

Prayer, when combined with fasting, is brilliant because instead of relying on personal power, we can connect to God and draw on Divine power. This is exactly what Chávez did. And he saw staggering results. Chávez understood his people and recognized the cultural values that united them. "*Abuelita* Theology," *La Virgen de Guadalupe* (iconography), penitence, prayer, fasting, and pilgrimage were the heart language of the *Campesinos*.

> Chávez believed that one way to break through the fear that many farmworkers felt was to talk to them in a religious language that they understood and respected. Thus, Chávez frequently invoked the teachings of the Catholic Church, and Pope John XXIII on economic

---

30. Martinez, "La Marcha."

justice and the rights of the world's agricultural workers to live lives of dignity.[31]

The church needs to understand the lesson from César Chávez if we want to effectively minister to them.

V. ÓSCAR ROMERO

Óscar Romero was a Central American archbishop from El Salvador. He was born into a poor and humble family with no special privileges. At the age of twenty-five, he was ordained into the ministry. During his ministry, El Salvador was in the midst of a violent civil war.

> Over and over, he challenged those in power to care for their countrymen, he encouraged the campesinos to pray, to live more truly by the vision of the New Testament, and he reminded his entire audience of how Jesus came to earth in poverty, enduring the pain and humiliation of the cross before the triumph of his resurrection. Because Christ knows all the suffering on earth . . . we can believe in and work for his kingdom on earth.[32]

Even when he was appointed as archbishop of San Salvador, the capital of El Salvador, his basic message did not change. Romero maintained his belief and preached that the good news of the gospel was for the poor and the oppressed. Romero's conviction was based on Matthew chapter 25.

> The face of Christ is among the sacks and baskets of the farmworkers;
> The face of Christ is among those who are tortured and mistreated in prisons;
> The face of Christ is dying of hunger in the children who have nothing to eat;
> The face of Christ is in the poor who ask the church for their voice to be heard.

---

31. Thompson and Wiggins, *Human Cost of Food*, 260.
32. Romero, *Scandal of Redemption*, 1, 2.

How can the church deny their request when it is Christ who is telling us to speak for him?[33]

Romero's Central American Catholicism was very much an institutional one. His ministry used the Catholic belief and traditions as practiced within the Catholic Church itself. As an archbishop, he emphasized *La Misa* (the eucharist) and baptism as a means of evangelism and nurture. This was the common ground between him and his people.

Sacramental spirituality is the spirituality that is expressed through the sacraments. The sacraments can be understood as conduits of God's grace. They give us the strength to live a holy life and mature in our faith. Within the Roman Catholic Church, there are seven sacraments: baptism, eucharist, confirmation, reconciliation/confession, anointing of the sick, holy orders or ordinations, and marriage. Most Protestants recognize only baptism and the eucharist, or the Lord's Supper, as sacraments or ordinances.

Liturgy professor James F. White referred to baptism as "the sacrament of equality."[34] When I was a pastor in Fort Worth, Texas, I had the experience of reaching out to Hispanic Catholics in the neighborhood. Normally, people from the *barrio* or Hispanic neighborhood would not enter a Methodist church. However, one day a young woman visited and asked if we would be willing to baptize her baby girl. Her daughter was scheduled to have surgery and she was desperate for her to be baptized before the procedure. We had a conversation and set the day and time for the baptism. This family had a high regard and belief in the sacraments. They understood that in baptism not only did their daughter receive the blessing of the church, but she was received equally into the family of God.

Óscar Romero was assassinated on March 24, 1980, while leading *La Misa* in the chapel of the *Divina Providencia* hospital in San Salvador, El Salvador. The Gospel reading for that day was

---

33. Dennis et al., *Óscar Romero*, 35.
34. White, *Sacraments as God's Self Giving*, 96.

John 12:23-26, which speaks of a grain of wheat falling to the earth and dying.

> Archbishop Romero's last words beckoned his listeners to present their own lives as a sacrifice to others in the model of Christ. From the spiritual nourishment of the Eucharist, and Christian lives poured out in service, justice and peace would flow to the people of El Salvador. ... Whoever offers their life out of love for Christ ... will live like the seed that dies.[35]

VI. MICHAEL J. GORMAN

In his book *Cruciformity: Paul's Narrative Spirituality of the Cross*, Michael J. Gorman speaks about Paul's teaching to the Philippians and the meaning of a crucified life. Gorman identifies Paul's spirituality as a narrative spirituality. This type of spirituality tells a story about living a life with and for God. It is an experiential representation of the embodiment of the cross, which is best expounded in the book of Galatians.

> For through the law I died to the law, so that I might live to God. I have been crucified with Christ; and it is no longer I who live, but it is Christ who lives in me. And the life I now live in the flesh I live by faith, in the Son of God, who loved me and gave himself for me.[36]

Additionally, Gorman pinpoints this type of spirituality as cruciform. Paul's letters contain four fundamental patterns of cruciformity. These patterns clarify the intent and meaning of the term "cruciformity," coined by Gorman. They are characterized by faith, love, power, and hope. This four-part pattern of spirituality encourages us to integrate the following:

> A posture before God of radical self-offering (faith), to become a sort of Christ for others (love), to accept weakness as strength (power), and to yearn confidently for

35. Romero, *Brown Church*, 172.
36. Gal 2:19-20.

their own bodily resurrection and for the transformation of the entire creation (hope).[37]

We might think of a cruciform life as having our arms both stretched upwards toward God while also reaching out and embracing those around us. It is incumbent upon believers to live the story, embody the story, and tell the story of faith, love, power, and hope.[38]

VII. ELDIN VILLAFAÑE

In his book *Beyond Cheap Grace*, Eldin Villafañe asserts that the challenge for the church today is to have a Christian mindset that is willing to engage in the practice of self-emptying. That is, we must be willing to surrender our status, our privilege, and our control. Authentic Christian discipleship requires sacrifice and service. "The world looks at the church and wants to see in our lives the marks of the cross—not the search for comfort, prestige, power, or fame. Christian discipleship is costly."[39] Christians must present the gospel to the *Campesinos* and to all others through tangible acts of love and justice. As we live into God's calling to reach out and minister to our *Campesino* brothers and sisters, I share with you the following prayer.

> May God bless you with *discomfort* at easy answers, half-truths, and superficial relationships, so that you may live deep within your heart.
>
> May God bless you with *anger* at injustice, oppression, and exploitation of people, so that you may work for justice, freedom, and peace.
>
> May God bless you with *tears* to shed for those who suffer from pain, rejection, starvation, and war, so that you

---

37. Gorman, *Cruciformity*, 400.
38. Gorman, *Cruciformity*, 367.
39. Villafañe, *Beyond Cheap Grace*, 15.

may reach out your hand to comfort them and to turn their pain into joy.

And may God bless you with enough *foolishness* to believe that you can make a difference in this world, so that you can do what others claim cannot be done.[40]

As Christians we must, by necessity, demonstrate the gospel by identifying with the people, regardless of whether they are sitting in the pews of our various houses of worship or are hunched over in the fields harvesting produce. Jesus became like one of us. He became flesh to bring us salvation. From the apostle Paul, we learn that it is essential to our ministry that we relate to all people, including the *Campesinos*.

> For though I am free with respect to all, I have made myself a slave to all, so that I might win more of them. To the Jews I became as a Jew, in order to win Jews. To those under the law I became as one under the law (though I myself am not under the law) so that I might win those under the law. To those outside the law I became as one outside the law (though I am not free from God's law but am under Christ's law) so that I might win those outside the law. To the weak I became weak, so that I might win the weak. I have become all things to all people, that I might by all means save some.[41]

In other words, to thrive in ministry is to become relatable to our charge. We need to become one with the people.

CONCLUSION

Piers Plowman, Tomás Rivera, César Chávez, and Óscar Romero all share something very intimate with the *Campesinos*. It is their strong connection with the land. We ought to acknowledge and celebrate the strength of character and determination of the *Campesinos*. Using the analogy of *La Mesa Campesina*, we can

---

40. Villafañe, *Beyond Cheap Grace*, 81.
41. 1 Cor 9:19–22.

invite them to bring their *taburetes* and dine with their *compañeros*—Piers Plowman, Tomás Rivera, César Chávez, and Óscar Romero. In other words, they will be in a faith community that recognizes and honors the cultural values and spiritual resources that nurture them. May the kingdom of God thrive wherever we plow, plant, and water God's good word. And may it be said of us like it was said of St. Augustine:

> But the city of God continued to flourish wherever the ideas of Augustine and his predecessors fell like seeds into fertile soil, producing abundant fruit in nations and countries of which they had never heard. Their voices continued to resound through Christian centuries to come, enriching the spiritual understanding and encouraging the piety of future generations which sought after the deep things of God.[42]

In chapter 4, we will discuss how *La Mesa Campesina* can be a rich feast that celebrates the lives of the *Campesinos* and acknowledges their life experiences of pilgrimage, mortality, family, prayer, and sacraments. These elements will be intertwined in a curriculum for teaching about *Campesinos*.

---

42. Burgess, *Holy Spirit*, 197.

Chapter 4

Teaching about *Campesinos*

THIS CHAPTER WILL COVER the curriculum teaching about *Campesinos*. The learning outcome is to raise awareness and empathy in the local churches. This tool will help guide pastors and laity as they begin their outreach to the often overlooked and underestimated strangers among them.

ORGANIZATION

This study is organized according to Richard R. Osmer's *Practical Theology: An Introduction*. In his book, Osmer lays out his pastoral theology of congregational leadership in four tasks.

1. The descriptive-empirical task.
2. The interpretive task.
3. The normative task.
4. The pragmatic task.[1]

Through these four tasks, Osmer is directing our attention to four key questions we should be asking about our ministry and

---

1. Osmer, *Practical Theology*, 4.

our congregants. What's happening? Why is it happening? What should be happening? And how can we help?[2]

The first task is the descriptive-empirical task which involves priestly listening.[3] Priests always had a significant function in Israel's worship of God. For example, the priests would accept and offer up the people's sacrifices to God. "Then the priest shall turn the whole into smoke on the altar as a burnt offering."[4] By making themselves available to the people by listening to them, a relationship would ensue. As trust in that relationship grew, the people were more open to being drawn closer to the presence of God. They were more willing to learn about God and his love and what God expected of them. Priestly listening by necessity involves being present in their lives. We ought to know the particularities that are occurring in the congregation's life so that we might effectively minister to them. Knowing what is happening in a person's life can only be achieved through active, nonjudgmental listening. We must spend time with the people, in this case, with the *Campesinos*. According to Leander Keck,

> The pastor is truly a priest when the prayer articulates the situation of the congregation through his or her prayer. For this to happen, one must listen to the people and establish a critical identity with them. . . . To pray on their behalf, one must enter into their lives to the point that one begins to feel what they feel, yet without losing one's identity.[5]

The second task is the interpretive task, which involves sagely wisdom.[6] This task involves allowing the Holy Spirit to guide us as leaders or pastors as we in turn guide others in how to live for God when difficulties arise. How do we interpret biblical teachings to the *Campesinos* when they ask, "Why is this happening?" From the book of Ecclesiastes, we know that God is sovereign over all

---

2. Osmer, *Practical Theology*, 4.
3. Osmer, *Practical Theology*, 31.
4. Lev 1:9b.
5. Keck, *Bible in the Pulpit*, 62.
6. Osmer, *Practical Theology*, 82.

creation, including time. God encompasses the past, the present, and the future, and nothing happens outside of his knowledge and control.

> For everything there is a season, and a time for every matter under heaven:
> a time to be born, and a time to die;
> a time to plant, and a time to pluck up what is planted;
> a time to kill, and a time to heal;
> a time to break down, and a time to build up;
> a time to weep, and a time to laugh;
> a time to mourn, and a time to dance;
> a time to throw away stones, and a time to gather stones together;
> a time to embrace, and a time to refrain from embracing;
> a time to seek, and a time to lose;
> a time to keep, and a time to throw away;
> a time to tear, and a time to sew;
> a time to keep silence, and a time to speak;
> a time to love, and a time to hate;
> a time for war, and a time for peace.[7]

These conversations are important and can only occur when a level of trust and openness has been established.

Osmer's third task is the normative task of prophetic discernment.[8] In this task, we want to know what is happening. In ancient Israel, the prophets were God's mouthpiece. Whenever Israel strayed from their covenant with God, God would send a prophet to point out their lapse in obedience. The prophet's role was to announce God's judgment while also giving them hope if they repented and returned to fulfilling their part of the covenant.

> Discernment is the activity of seeking God's guidance amid the circumstances, events, and decisions of life. To discern means to sift through and sort out, much as a prospector must sift out the dross to find nuggets of gold. It also means to weigh the evidence before reaching

---

7. Eccl 3:1–8.
8. Osmer, *Practical Theology*, 132.

a decision, much as a judge listens to all evidence in a case before reaching a verdict.[9]

The spiritual gift of discernment allows leaders, clergy, and laity to help others hear God's word and more importantly to obey it and apply it to the circumstances of their lives. This task investigates God's will for our present reality. In other words, how do we interpret our everyday situations?

Lastly, the fourth task is the pragmatic task or servant leadership.[10] This is where we determine what our leadership style or function is. It also asks the all-important question: How can we help? A servant leader focuses on the needs of others before considering their own. This type of leader is more concerned about the people they are ministering to than they are about what they can gain from them. Servant leaders want to serve rather than to be served. Jesus teaches us that we serve God truly only when we serve others. This is evidenced in the following passage: "For the Son of Man came not to be served but to serve, and to give his life a ransom for many."[11] Furthermore, to serve effectively we must listen deeply. For it is in listening that we learn when and how to serve others.

According to Osmer there are three forms of leadership: task-oriented, transactional, and transforming.[12] The task-oriented leader can be described as one whose focus is on leading the group or the organization. A transactional leader is when a leader is using trade-offs to influence people. For example, a transactional ministry with the *Campesinos* might include providing food and water, clothing, etc., in the hope that an opportunity might present itself to offer the word of God. Lastly, there is transforming leadership. This is when the leader can guide a group to a big change. In this case, it is presenting the gospel of Jesus Christ for

---

9. Osmer, *Practical Theology*, 137.
10. Osmer, *Practical Theology*, 175.
11. Mark 10:45.
12. Osmer, *Practical Theology*, 178.

the transformation of the world. All three leadership styles are important and necessary in a ministry, especially in a new renewal movement.

Osmer's model helps us address some necessary questions as we look to reach the *Campesinos*. First, we need to be aware of what is happening with *Campesinos*. Second, why is it happening? Third, what should be happening? And lastly, how can we help? Specifically, how might we help them in coming to a relationship with God?

Data Collection

The methodology for this project will include both quantitative and qualitative data to develop a descriptive profile of the migrant population. The quantitative data will come from government resources such as the Michigan Department of Civil Rights, the Michigan Department of Education, the Texas Education Agency, the US Bureau of Labor Statistics, and the US Census. The qualitative data will come from in-person oral interviews of migrants, clergy, a retired bishop of the United Methodist Church, and laity responding to questions that I will prepare in advance. Letters of permission and consent will be used to protect the privacy of interviewees. I will record these interviews using digital technology. Their responses will be transcribed into a Word document for coding. The raw data will be stored securely offline. The results will be graphically displayed in the appendix of the study.

Scheme

I accomplished the pragmatic aspect of my research by developing a six-week Bible study. I facilitated the 1.5-hour lessons and conversations every Wednesday evening beginning July 13, 2022, and concluding on August 17, 2022. These studies were held at La Trinidad United Methodist Church, 306 E. Gonzales St., Seguin, Texas, with the permission of the pastor, Rev. Nohemí Ramirez.

The group consisted of eleven to thirteen participants. It was comprised of one to three males with the remainder of the group being females. They ranged in age from eighteen up to ninety-two years old. It is also important to say that I had no previous knowledge, acquaintances, connections, or friendships with any of the participants.

LESSON I: INTRODUCTION

July 13, 2022

The first lesson served as a time for introductions. I designed this first evening as a time for all of us to get acquainted. I began by sharing my name, background, topic, and reason for my interest in this subject matter. Everyone had an opportunity to introduce themselves by stating their names and communicating any experience or personal knowledge they might have had with or about *Campesinos*.

In the first meeting, I explained to them what to expect over the course of this study. As this group was already accustomed to sharing a fellowship meal before their study, we continued with the tradition of eating from six o'clock to six thirty p.m. with the lesson immediately following the meal. Because the subject matter focused on the very poor, the meals we shared were in line with the food of the poor. For example, we ate bean tacos, *fideo* (vermicelli noodles in a chicken broth flavored with onion, garlic, and tomatoes), *tacos al vapor* (steamed corn tortillas stuffed with precooked fillings), and *calabacita* (sauteed chayote, zucchini, and yellow squash, corn, tomatoes, and peppers). We tried to honor and demonstrate respect to the *Campesinos* by not just hearing and learning from their stories but also eating the kind of meals they themselves would consume daily.

Singing

We started each lesson by joining our voices together in singing the hymn entitled "Vamos Todos al Banquete / Let Us Go Now to the Banquet." The following is the chorus of that hymn.

Vamos todos al banquete,
A la mesa de la creación.
Cada cual con su taburete,
Tiene un puesto y una misión.

Let us go now to the banquet,
To the feast of the universe.
The table's set and a place is waiting;
Come, ev'ry one, with your gifts to share.[13]

The second stanza of this Salvadoran hymn tells us that God invites all the poor to this common table. At this table, no one is a hoarder, and everyone has something to put into their tortilla. What we can ascertain from this is that at the Lord's table, the wealthy do not eat more than the poor. The *taburete*, which the chorus speaks of, is a small stool that the farmers carried with them. This hymn, therefore, communicates to us that everyone, including the *Campesinos*, has a place and a mission in the church. What a beautiful message to learn that at God's table we are all equal. All of us ought to be working and struggling together for the good of humanity. Therefore, because God's banquet is ready, let's each grab our own *taburete* and join the festivities.

The Posters

After due diligence had been given to the eating and singing, we proceeded to the evening's lesson. As a means of introducing the focus of my ministry, I displayed five posters from the Smithsonian Institution Traveling Exhibition Service entitled *Bittersweet Harvest: The Bracero Program, 1942–1964*. We looked at each poster

---

13. Cuéllar, "Vamos Todos al Banquete."

and talked about them, and each participant had an opportunity to reflect on them. The posters included:

1. *La Historia* / The Story.

This poster depicts the narrative through a picture of the guest agricultural farmworkers traveling in a caravan from Mexico to the United States. The braceros filled in during and after the war years. "Mexican farm workers were brought to the United States in accordance with the agreement between our two governments . . . are contributing their skill and their toil to the production of vitally needed food."[14]

2. *El Viaje* / The Journey.

The image in this poster is particularly disturbing. The men are lined up and sprayed with the pesticide DDT. "They sprayed us like rats, like insects. We left covered in powder."[15]

3. *La Cosecha* / The Harvest.

The picture on this poster reveals workers bent over in half, harvesting crops like sugar beets and lettuce. "That's where we encountered *el cortito*, or what's called the short-handled hoe. And for sure, that is where I shed my tears."[16]

4. *Amargo Dulce* / Bittersweet.

This poster shows a bracero reading a letter as he sits on an old cot with nothing more than a too-short flimsy mattress in a dirty room with dirty walls. The braceros endured backbreaking work

---

14. Franklin Delano Roosevelt, 32nd president of the United States, in *Bittersweet Harvest*, 1.
15. Isaías Sánchez, ex-bracero, in *Bittersweet Harvest*, 4.
16. Jose Natividad Alva Medina, ex-bracero, in *Bittersweet Harvest*, 4.

and substandard housing with limited water, heat, and sanitary facilities so they could benefit financially. The money they earned they sent to their families back in Mexico. "As a kid, I couldn't understand . . . why didn't [my father] stay here?"[17]

5. La Comunidad / The Community.

The picture in this poster portrays a family including a grandmother, mother, and children nicely dressed probably getting ready for church. The room in the house has a picture of Jesus and of *La Virgen de Guadalupe*. "We sent money to our families in Mexico so [they could] . . . eat better, dress better, and live better while we were in the U.S."[18] Whereas the braceros, while in the US, formed their own communities to help each other adjust to life in the camps. Some of the towns reached out to the braceros and held social events like dances and churches offered worship services for them in Spanish.

LESSON 2: IDENTITY AND COMPASSION

July 20, 2022

The foundation of lesson two is the story of Moses as found in the book of Exodus, chapter 2. To facilitate the study and guide our discussions I developed and distributed worksheets to each student every week. Each worksheet consisted of three parts: 1. Story, 2. Group Discussion, and 3. Imagine Action.

On the evening of July 20, 2022, I began by giving some background information on Moses. In the first verse of chapter 2, we learn that Moses's parents were Levites, but their names are not mentioned. Their names, however, are revealed later in the book of Exodus. "Amram married Jochebed . . . and she bore him Aaron

---

17. Felipe Flores, son of a bracero, in *Bittersweet Harvest*, 4.
18. Ignacio Gómez, ex-bracero, in *Bittersweet Harvest*, 4.

and Moses."[19] The Levites have a special status among the tribes of Israel as they are the priests and assistants in worship in the holy temple.

> For they observed your word, and kept your covenant.
> They teach Jacob your ordinances, and Israel your law;
> they place incense before you, and whole burnt offerings on your altar.[20]

By introducing Moses in this way, the writer of the book of Exodus is suggesting that Moses's Levitical status is suitable for a future leader and lawgiver of Israel. Additionally, Moses's rescue and his upbringing in pharaoh's house is a signal that God has special intentions for him and that we as the reader should trust him as a leader. Moreover, Moses's preservation in the Nile River, which is teeming with crocodiles, suggests and echoes the story of Noah and the flood and God's plan to preserve his people. The name Moses in Hebrew means "the one who draws out."[21] God is the one who delivered Moses. This is also a clue to Moses's future role of drawing the oppressed Israelites out of Egypt. People of every age who are weighed down, demoralized, and exploited can identify with the Hebrew people as they too endured slave labor. The Bible speaks against the mistreatment of orphans, the poor, and the strangers. Our hearts should ache for the deliverance and wholeness of all the oppressed. This is especially true for the *Campesinos*. With each harvest season, the family faces the devastating reality of uprooting their family, leaving behind their home, friends, school, church, and community. They desire deliverance and wholeness. They want their lives to have happy endings. The *Campesinos* want hope and purpose. This is where the church can step in and give them the hope of Jesus Christ.

---

19. Exod 6:20.
20. Deut 33:9c–10.
21. Exod 2:10.

A. Story: Moses

Members of the Bible study group voluntarily took turns reading aloud the assigned biblical passage of Exodus, chapter 2. As we read the chapter, I asked them to look and listen for evidence of a relationship between Moses and the Hebrew slaves. I followed with the question, "What is the message of Exodus?" As the discussion unfurled and developed, I asked them to look for Moses's identity and compassion and also look for God's identity and compassion. My next question for the group was, "Who is God and what does God do for Moses and the Israelites in this portion of Scripture?"

B. Group Discussion

As we transitioned from the story to a time of discussion, I asked the group to reflect on Moses's experience. We witness the shift in his life from being a member of pharaoh's household and residing in the palace to being homeless and living in the open fields of Midian.

I offered the following statements and questions to support and guide our dialogue.

1. The Israelites suffered and were oppressed by the social system of that day. How do these systems come into being? How can we change them?
2. Moses's call and response are significant to the Exodus story. Describe a time when you felt God speaking or calling you to action.
3. What is it about being a Christian that moves us to weep with those who suffer and hope with those who despair?

C. Imagine Action

The last section of our study is what I call "Imagine Action." This is where I encouraged the group to move from just talking to stepping out in faith and creatively and with purpose considering what they might be able to accomplish for the *Campesinos*. Prayer is always good and needed; however, I suggested they do something tangible for the *Campesinos*. In conclusion, I asked them to consider the story of Moses in the context of the *Campesinos*. I followed up with the final question of the evening, "What actions of mission could they imagine for the local church?"

LESSON 3: WORK AND JUSTICE

July 27, 2022

Before the third lesson, I telephoned each group member a few days before our class meeting to give them their homework assignment. I asked them to read the entire book of Amos in preparation for the class Bible study. Surprisingly, everyone was excited and willing to comply with my request.

The topic for this lesson was "Work and Justice" and together we examined the writings of the prophet Amos. I gave a brief overview of the prophet, describing him as a shepherd from a small town in Tekoa in Judah who worked hard and earned his living as a livestock breeder and a dresser of sycamore trees. In other words, he raised sheep and collected figs. But Amos was more than a simple man from a simple village, he was a man who exercised his gifts of obedience, discipline, hard work, and faith in God. So, God acted through Amos, elevating him, and leaving for all of us a long-lasting legacy. We then turned our attention to our worksheets.

A. Story: Amos

I asked the group what themes surfaced for them while reading the book of Amos. What themes could you identify? They were all very eager to offer their responses. The overwhelming response to the question was "justice." As we continued with our dialogue, I explained that Amos was concerned about the justice of opportunity.

When he went to Israel it was a time of unprecedented prosperity and unlimited power in Israel. Amos was pleading for "justice to roll down like waters and righteousness like an ever-flowing stream."[22] The rich were taking advantage of the poor. This is still happening today. Why should the rich be able to get a loan for 6 percent while the poor often are left with no alternative but to enter the doors of a Payday loan office to obtain their loans? These establishments charge interest rates of around 300 percent! These companies are taking advantage of the poor and desperate people. The church needs to stand up for the poor, the *Campesinos*, and others who feel they have no alternative but to do business with them. Justice is one of the themes of Amos along with work, judgment, injustice, the sins of God's people, and repentance.

B. Group Discussion

For this discussion, we examined six different passages categorized into two sections. In the first grouping or section, we read the Scriptures to identify the sins against our neighbors.

Section 1: Sins against Our Neighbors

Amos 2:6–8

> Thus says the Lord: for three transgressions of Israel, and for four, I will not revoke the punishment; because they sell the righteous for silver, and the needy for a pair of sandals—they who trample the head of the poor into the dust of the earth, and push the afflicted out of the way; father and son go in to the same girl, so that my holy name is profaned; they lay themselves down beside every altar on garments taken in pledge; and in the house of their God they drink wine bought with fines they imposed.[23]

---

22. Amos 5:24.
23. Amos 2:6–8.

This passage speaks of how the poor and afflicted were treated by Israel, with contempt rather than kindness. These verses of Scripture not only reveal how the Israelites oppressed the poor but also describe their vulgarity and profanity.

Amos 4:1–3

> Hear this word, you cows of Bashan who are on Mount Samaria, who oppress the poor, who crush the needy, who say to their husbands, "Bring something to drink!" The Lord God has sworn by his holiness: The time is surely coming upon you, when they shall take you away with hooks, even the last of you with fishhooks. Through breaches in the wall you shall leave, each one straight ahead; and you shall be flung out into Harmon, says the Lord.[24]

In this chapter, the people of Israel are threatened with calamities for their continued oppression of the poor. Amos is talking to the women of Samaria. Perhaps we are insulted or even chuckle at his words. But what is going on in this passage? Amos was talking to the female social elite. The cows of Bashan refer to the well-fed women. The emphasis is not a negative reflection of their weight. On the contrary, an overweight wealthy woman was a good thing because it meant that she would bear healthy babies as compared to an underweight, malnourished peasant woman. Amos was not just calling them well-fed; he was calling them lazy. Laziness is the more loathsome vice. Amos was calling them lazy cows.

This was the culture of the elites of Samaria, both male and female. Amos zeroes in on the women to reveal how that ungodly character was manifested in their comportment. The lack of good character is revealed in two ways: 1. They oppress the helpless and crush the poor. They are elitist women who cannot be bothered to think about those beneath their station, and, 2. They are lazy rather than hardworking. They just lie about and call on their husbands to bring them something to drink. They are like lazily grazing cows.

---

24. Amos 4:1–3.

This is the opposite of the virtuous woman who "opens her hand to the poor and reaches out her hands to the needy."[25] This passage in the book of Proverbs highlights good character. Furthermore, good character is not gender-specific; it applies to both men and women.

Amos 5:10–13

> They hate the one who reproves in the gate, and they abhor the one who speaks the truth. Therefore, because you trample on the poor and take from them levies of grain, you have built houses of hewn stone, but you shall not live in them; you have planted pleasant vineyards, but you shall not drink their wine. For I know how many are your transgressions, and how great are your sins— you who afflict the righteous, who take a bribe, and push aside the needy in the gate. Therefore, the prudent will keep silent in such a time; for it is an evil time.[26]

Amos once again accuses Israel of practicing injustice which violates God's covenant with Israel. He calls them out and says that God will judge his covenant people. Judgment will fall on Israel because their culture has deteriorated, and they no longer love the truth. Moreover, they lacked integrity.

The gate in the city was the spot in Israel where judges or rulers would often administer justice. This is where they would hold court. But Israel had come to despise justice. The people were not seeking the truth. They only wanted their own way regardless of whether it involved lies. Israel had broken her covenant with God by trampling on the poor, seizing their grain, taking bribes, and ignoring the needy.

---

25. Prov 31:20.
26. Amos 5:10–13.

Amos 6:4–7

> Alas for those who lie on beds of ivory, and lounge on their couches, and eat lambs from the flock, and calves from the stall; who sing idle songs to the sound of the harp, and like David improvise on instruments of music; who drink wine from bowls, and anoint themselves with the finest oils, but are not grieved over the ruin of Joseph! Therefore, they shall now be the first to go into exile, and the revelry of the loungers shall pass away.[27]

This is a portrait of a life of faith that has gone horribly wrong. The Israelites are at ease because they are confident that no harm will happen to them. Amos proceeds by saying, "Look around friends. What do you see in the neighboring countries? Has anyone escaped the devastation? Why do you think you will be any different?"[28]

Our passage beginning with verse 4 speaks of the luxuries that the Israelites were enjoying. Luxuries such as sleeping on beds of ivory and eating meat, drinking wine, and singing idle songs. Amos was speaking directly to those in power in Jerusalem and Samaria. Normally the people slept on the floor, on thin, woven mats and their diet consisted primarily of fruits, grains, and vegetables with little meat consumed. It was the powerful leaders who were taxing the poor and then using the money to keep themselves in the life of luxury that they had become accustomed to. These were the leaders whom God had entrusted with power and authority to fulfill his mission. This was not to be for their own benefit. Their mission was to cultivate the faith of God's people. Instead, they abused their power for their own gain.

Amos 8:4–6

This is the last passage in the section on sins against our neighbors.

> Hear this, you that trample on the needy, and bring to ruin the poor of the land, saying, "When will the new

27. Amos 6:4–7.
28. Amos 6:1–3.

moon be over so that we may sell grain; and the sabbath, so that we may offer wheat for sale? We will make the ephah small and the shekel great, and practice deceit with false balances, buying the poor for silver and the needy for a pair of sandals, and selling the sweepings of the wheat."[29]

Once again, as in the previous passages of scriptures we have reviewed, the Israelites continue to trample and oppress the poor. Amos exposes the Israelites' treatment of the most vulnerable in society. This ruthless behavior has become rampant. Scripture further informs us of their plotting and scheming during the holy times of the Sabbath and other sacred observances. Instead of worshiping God, they are devising ways to keep the poor in debt slavery. Their worship, mingled with injustice, has become unacceptable to God.

> The time is surely coming says the Lord God, when I will send a famine on the land; not a famine of bread, or a thirst for water, but of hearing the words of the Lord. They shall wander from sea to sea, and from north to east; they shall run to and fro, seeking the word of the Lord, but they shall not find it.[30]

Section 2: Acceptable Worship

Amos 5:21–24

In the second section of our Group Discussion, we examined the following passage.

> I hate, I despise your festivals, and I take no delight, in your solemn assemblies. Even though you offer me your burnt offerings and grain offerings, I will not accept them; and the offerings of well-being of your fatted animals I will not look upon. Take away from me the noise of your songs; I will not listen to the melody of your harps. But

29. Amos 8:4–6.
30. Amos 8:11–12.

let justice roll down like waters, and righteousness like an ever-flowing stream.[31]

This text communicates to us that worship and life must go hand in hand. You cannot separate or compartmentalize the two. If we do not take care of the less fortunate, God does not want our praises and prayers. Acceptable worship is determined by what happens outside the sanctuary as much as by what happens inside of it. We, like the Israelites, will be judged by this basic criterion: How well are the less fortunate members of our society being cared for? The final question for the Group Discussion was "What does God want from us?" After listening to various responses, we proceeded to the third section of the worksheet.

C. Imagine Action

In this closing section, I asked the group to think about the implications of Amos's story in the context of the *Campesinos'* life, experience, and treatment. I then raised the following question for reflection and a time of dialogue. "What action items can we imagine for the local church?"

LESSON 4: *FAMILIA* AND PILGRIMAGE

August 3, 2022

For this week's lesson, we had two stories. The first was *Piers Plowman*. This is a poem written by William Langland. The second story is about César Chávez. The organization for this class was the same as the previous two classes: 1. Story, 2. Group Discussion, and 3. Imagine Action. As with the previous lesson I provided handouts in advance for each student as reading homework in preparation for the class.

---

31. Amos 5:21–24.

A. Story: *Piers Plowman*

All the class members arrived having read the prologue to this fourteenth-century medieval English poem. The poem is a presentation of Christian history via dream visions. It is these visions that guide the reader through William Langland's spiritual journey. I focused on the prologue because it is here that one can best grasp humanity's situation as seen through the eyes of Langland. He had a series of dream visions on his quest to live a good Christian life. Along the way, Langland meets different characters who represent both his external and internal world, as well as the different social and economic classes of medieval England. Through this journey he learns about himself and his own physical needs. As the characters travel together, they fight with each other about God, the church, money, and how to live. This experience is not much different than what happens in our churches today. The character of interest for this evening's study is named Piers. He is a humble plowman. He is also the one that knows the way to Truth and will guide the pilgrims through a plowing field. Piers represents a model of Christian behavior that stresses the importance of performing good works. Piers offers to help guide the people if they will help him plow his field. He substitutes agricultural labor for pilgrimage. Of course, not everyone can or even wants to work. Those who are unable to work are taken care of through Christian charity. Those who refuse to work are dealt with through the character named Hunger. This is a natural solution that works to motivate the idlers long enough to gather the harvest. This poem explicitly connects work with Christian virtue.

The poem opens with Langland wandering the world as a hermit. One day he lies down by a stream and falls into a deep sleep and dreams an extraordinary dream. What does he see in this dream? He sees a field full of people—all kinds of people from all walks of life. These individuals were totally oblivious to their close proximity to heaven and hell. Langland noticed that humanity was comprised of those who seek to do good and those who are more interested in being self-serving, deceitful, or having a ravenous appetite for all things physical. The second group appears to be more concerned with their materialistic needs and desires rather than with their spiritual welfare. William Langland draws the conclusion that hard work, honest living, and charity are what will lead the pilgrim to their encounter with Truth, that is, with God. Piers Plowman equates plowing with pilgrimage. His act of sowing is his pilgrimage. This can be the same for the *Campesinos*. The dedicated work of their hands is nothing to be ashamed of. In fact, it can be the instrument that ushers them into a relationship with Jesus Christ.

B. Group Discussion

For our Group Discussion, I prompted them with the following question for our consideration and time of dialogue.

How does this poem apply to experiences of spiritual pilgrimage?

C. Imagine Action

The closing section is a time to reflect on the evening's discussion and to collectively plan a course of action to minister to the *Campesinos*. I invited the group to consider the following two questions to facilitate this section.

1. What are the connections between Piers Plowman and the *Campesino* experience?
2. What can our church do to facilitate a spiritual experience for *Campesinos*?

D. Story: César Chávez

I shared César Chávez's story with the Wednesday night Bible study group. This is the same story I mentioned in chapter 3. In essence, Chávez and his family were *Campesino* workers. Their life, as well as those of other farmworkers, was too familiar with injustice. I believe he was called by God to speak up against the powerful leaders of the agricultural business. Evidence of this is seen in a "Letter from Delano," which César Chávez wrote to E. L. Barr, president of the California Grape and Tree Fruit League, stating,

> This letter does not express all that is in my heart, Mr. Barr. But if it says nothing else it says that we do not hate you or rejoice to see your industry destroyed, we hate the agribusiness system that seeks to keep us enslaved, and we shall overcome and change it not by retaliation or bloodshed but by a determined nonviolent struggle carried on by those masses of farm workers who intend to be free and human.[32]

E. Group Discussion

After familiarizing ourselves with Chávez's story I asked two questions to stimulate discussion.

1. What is significant about César Chávez's work ethic and belief system?
2. What were the Christian teachings/observances that he put into practice in working with the farmworkers?

F. Imagine Action

As we concluded the study, I asked them to employ their imaginations, as we do every week, to envision a plan of action. The question for their consideration was as follows:

Using the information we learned from César Chávez, what can we as a church do to help the *Campesinos*?

---

32. Chávez, "Letter from Delano."

La Mesa Campesina

LESSON 5: LIFE AND DEATH

August 10, 2022

For this evening's study, we reviewed two stories on two different individuals, Tomás Rivera and Óscar Romero. Both individuals were discussed in detail in chapter 3. Before we dove into our official class format, I showed some vignettes from a film called *The Harvest [La Cosecha]*.[33] The clips were part of a documentary that followed the lives of several *Campesino* workers comprised of teenagers and their parents. The stories are real, depicting the struggles the families and children experienced.

A. Story: Tomás Rivera

Tomás Rivera understood the reality of *Campesino* life, and he hated it. His anger and frustration about their status in life are evident in his book *Y No se lo Tragó la Tierra*. We reviewed a previously distributed handout. The handout was an excerpt from his book that gives a clear insight into his understanding and thoughts about God.

B. Group Discussion

The discussion included thoughts, experiences, and memories evoked by the vignettes at the beginning of the class. After that, we moved into the questions pertaining to Tomás Rivera.

1. What is happening in this story?
2. What is Tomás's perspective?
3. What is his mother's perspective?
4. What is the takeaway from this story?

---

33. Romano, *Harvest*.

C. Imagine Action

Again, my goal was to help the study group make a connection between the various stories, the *Campesinos*, and the church. Therefore, I prompted the class with the following questions:

1. Is there a connection between the *Campesinos* and Tomás Rivera? What is it?
2. What action can the church take to address Rivera's issue while ministering to the *Campesinos*?

D. Story: Óscar Romero

I decided to begin the study by showing a portion of the film on the life and work of Archbishop Óscar Romero.[34] I felt that this would be the most effective and comprehensive way of familiarizing the group with this humble, determined, and courageous servant of God. Afterward, we read his final homily based on a passage from the Gospel of John.

> Jesus answered them, "The hour has come for the Son of Man to be glorified. Very truly, I tell you, unless a grain of wheat falls into the earth and dies, it remains just a single grain; but if it dies, it bears much fruit. Those who love their life lose it, and those who hate their life in this world will keep it for eternal life. Whoever serves me must follow me, and where I am, there will my servant be also. Whoever serves me, the Father will honor."[35]

It was at the end of the homily when Romero was at the altar table lifting the host and the cup that the fateful shot rang out killing him.

---

34. Duigan, *Romero*.
35. John 12:23–26.

E. Group Discussion

1. What are the differences between the two reading assignments of Tomás Rivera and Óscar Romero?
2. What lesson can we learn from Óscar Romero that will be beneficial in our work, our connections, and our relationships with the poor?

F. Imagine Action

To conclude the evening's discussion, as had been our practice throughout the study, I asked them a final question:

Taking into consideration tonight's readings, what kind of action can the church embrace to minister to the needs of the *Campesinos*?

LESSON 6: *LA MESA CAMPESINA*

August 17, 2022

Throughout our time together we heard the voices, the concerns, and the struggles of the *Campesinos*. We also witnessed the actions of persons who addressed their needs, both physical and spiritual. Some of us know firsthand what their day-to-day existence is like because we, too, have experienced it. With these realities in mind, let us reflect on our own lives and think about what we wish the church had done for us.

A. Bringing the Stories Together

This is the last study on the *peregrinación* or pilgrimage that I had with my fellow *Campesinos*. As we journeyed together, we prayed, we wept, we heard testimonies, we saw heartbreaking videos, and gazed upon posters of the braceros. Together we read scriptures from both the Old and New Testaments and acquainted ourselves with and gained some theological understanding from a variety of other readings. The readings included excerpts from César Chávez, Tomás Rivera, Óscar Romero, and *Piers Plowman*. All the readings were intended to open our hearts, our minds, and our arms to embrace our calling to minister to our fellow brothers and sisters, especially the *Campesinos*. Of course, this sounds all too serious; we also ate, sang, laughed, and became acquainted with one another. It is my prayer and most sincere hope that the church will continue to imagine an action of how to minister to the *Campesinos* of Seguin, Texas.

On this last gathering, we culminate with what I call *La Mesa Campesina*. We reflect on the gifts that each of the lesson's heroes brings to the table as a representative of the *Campesinos* as they encounter the liberating power of the gospel. Judaism's Passover has a Seder (literally means "order") plate with symbolic foods that retell the story of liberation. I, too, have chosen to tell this story through my own creation of a *Campesina* Seder plate utilizing our own symbolic foods. (See appendix for the photo of the *Campesina* Seder plate.)

LITURGY FOR *LA MESA CAMPESINA*

Leader:
Moses identified himself with his own people. He turned away from living a life of luxury where he could enjoy the finest food, clothing, and status to rejoin his family and his people. He worked alongside his people and chose to live with them. And he ate the food of the poor. In the case of *Campesinos*, the common food of the poor is beans. Therefore, beans are present at our table. We acknowledge this food because this is also our food.

People: Thank you, God, for your provision!

Leader:
The hardworking Amos was a livestock breeder and a dresser of sycamore or fig trees. Amos is a good example of a migrant worker because he was from Judah in the South and God called him to go

to the North to deliver God's message. Our *Campesinos* also travel from the South to the North. Amos had to go to a strange land where the people in the North knew that he was not one of them. To the table, Amos contributes lamb and figs. The lamb reminds us that Christ is our lamb, a sacrifice for our benefit.

People: For this we say, thank you, God!

Leader:
From Piers Plowman, we receive grain at our table. This grain is in the form of corn tortillas. Rice is also a grain, and it is present at our table in the style of Mexican rice.

People: For the humble tortillas and the rice we say, thank you, God!

Leader:
César Chávez is one of our *Campesinos*. His contribution to *La Mesa Campesina* is in the form of fruits and vegetables that he would have harvested. Our table holds lettuce, tomatoes, and cucumbers in the form of a salad. Grapes are also present because they represent the struggle against injustices. Strawberries, blueberries, and pineapple in our fresh fruit salad are also fruits harvested by our people.

People: For these fruits and vegetables that are picked by the very young and old we say, thank you, God!

Leader:
Tomás Rivera and Óscar Romero are two very different individuals. Yet, they share food that can be hard to swallow, hot chilies and cilantro. These two foods represent for us the experience of injustice and oppression. Both items are familiar and found at almost every Mexican table. The hot chilies represent the bitter times while the cilantro introduces a certain freshness and flavor that comes with new hope.

People: For the good and the bad times represented by these foods we say, thank you, God!

Leader:
The roast chicken that is present at our table tonight is a blessing because whether we are sick or in full health it is always a blessing to have a chicken. The poor know how to stretch a chicken. It can be fried, roasted, boiled in a soup, or made into a *guiso* (a stew-like dish). Chicken is a food that transcends status symbols. It is a dish that can be enjoyed by all.

People: And for this roasted chicken we say, thank you, God!

Leader/Prayer:
As we gaze upon and partake of each item of food let us be grateful to God not only for the food but for the calloused, rough, mahogany-colored hands that have harvested it. Our table is full to overflowing, our eyes dance with delight at the different colors, our noses are intrigued by the different aromas of each of the foods, and our mouths are enlivened by the delectable flavors that we will be tasting.

People: We are a blessed people because of the *Campesinos*. And together we say, thank you, God! Amen.

CONCLUSION

In the pilot program, the curriculum raised awareness of the plight of the *Campesinos* while yet imagining what it would be like for the church to reach them with the good news of Jesus Christ. My six-week study with the group from La Trinidad United Methodist Church was an experience that I will never forget. In the next chapter, I will discuss the rationale for establishing a ministry outreach to *Campesinos*.

Chapter 5

Reaching *Campesinos*

IN THIS CHAPTER, I will discuss my experience of promoting *Campesino* ministry to the Wednesday night Bible study group of La Trinidad United Methodist Church, Seguin, Texas. We faithfully remained together for the duration as we encountered the Holy Scriptures and other theological readings. The program included videos, posters, poetry, excerpts from novels, hymnody, and food in the sessions. All of these items were intended to remind us of our calling to love our neighbor and stimulate ministry to the *Campesinos*.

OBSERVATIONS

On the first evening of our study, I wasn't quite sure how the information would be received or for that matter how I would be received. Compared to their pastor and regular Bible teacher, I was a stranger. I displayed the five posters from the Smithsonian Institution traveling exhibition *Bittersweet Harvest* to introduce the subject matter.[1] To my surprise, this pleasant, reserved, quiet, and stoic group began to come to life. I witnessed a display of emotion that ranged from audible gasps, to remarks such as "I remember this," to tears streaming down their cheeks. Several participants

---
1. *Bittersweet Harvest*.

said, "I hadn't thought about this in years." They, of course, were reacting to the treatment and living conditions of the *Campesinos* as they recalled their own experiences as *Campesinos*. Most of the participants had long since buried those memories of their former life and were surprised at their own poignant display of emotion. The conversation was robust with 100 percent participation. Everyone was fully engaged and eager to learn what the following week's conversation would entail.

The second week's lesson focused on the biblical story of Moses. Together we read chapter 2 of Exodus. This chapter speaks of the rise and fall and the rise again of Moses. We learn of this hero's birth, his flight from Egypt to Midian, and his return as a national deliverer for the Israelites. As we entered our time of discussion, we examined Moses's relationship with the Hebrew slaves. We considered what his call from God might be and how Moses responded to that summons. I encouraged them to share about a time when they may have felt God tugging at their heart, prompting them into action. Several examples were raised as they shared how they had been moved at one time or another to help someone. For example, they referred to the "Blessing Box" located on the church property. This is a mini food pantry designed in the style of a Little Free Library. They fill this receptacle with shelf-stable food items instead of books. Anyone driving or walking by is free to take whatever they may need. Another way of caring for their neighbor is through the church's Prayer Garden. The Prayer Garden is a space on the church campus that is paved with bricks that form the shape of a Celtic cross. There are several benches along the perimeter of the cross where anyone and everyone is welcome to come, sit, meditate, or pray under the shade of the very large trees. A wooden prayer box mounted on a pole is situated near the edge of the property where you can leave your prayer requests. A small but faithful group of women and men collect these petitions every Monday morning to pray for those needs.

When I asked, "What is it about being a Christian that moves us to weep with those who suffer and hope with those who despair?" one of the participants, known to her peers as a woman of great faith, a believer in the power of prayer, and a devoted reader of the Bible, said, "We do this because this is what the Bible teaches." She was referring to the scripture that states, "Rejoice with those who rejoice, weep with those who weep."[2]

This group understood the concept of compassion and love for their neighbor and were already doing what they could imagine to do to extend the love of God to those around them. When I asked them to imagine what actions of mission their church could offer the *Campesinos*, they were very enthusiastic about the prospect. Yet, it was a challenge for them to come up with a concrete idea. I encouraged them to give it some regard through prayer and we would revisit it over the next few weeks.

In the third week, I centered our conversations around the book of Amos. Having read all nine chapters, the group was well prepared to enter the dialogue. When I asked for the theme of Amos, they were all willing to offer their answer. Of course, the overwhelming response was "justice." The group acknowledged other themes such as work, judgment, injustice, sin, and repentance. But they all wholeheartedly believed "justice" was the main theme.

As we proceeded to examine various selected passages, they were surprised by what they were reading in the Bible. They were not sure how to react to the verse that speaks of the "lazy cows of Bashan."[3] This was their first exposure to this text, and they were shocked. They didn't think something like this would be in the Bible. Some laughed, and others were embarrassed by what they read. However, they all agreed that laziness is a loathsome vice and something that Christians should avoid. When we compared the women of Samaria with the virtuous woman found in Prov 31, they said that God wants us to be like the woman in Proverbs. God wants us "to reach out our hands to the needy."[4] And this outreach includes the *Campesinos*.

2. Rom 12:15.
3. Amos 4:1–3.
4. Prov 31:20.

Reaching Campesinos

The Wednesday night group was taken aback when they read and heard with their own ears what God means by acceptable worship according to the fifth chapter of Amos, specifically the part of Scripture that says, "Take away from me the noise of your songs; I will not listen to the melody of your harps. But let justice roll down like waters, and righteousness like an ever-flowing stream."[5] As United Methodists, this group loves to sing their hymns. Any thought that God would not accept their songs of praise was troubling and a source of distress. As our conversation continued, they soon appreciated that worship is acceptable when we become imitators of God's justice and righteousness. One of the ladies said, "Well, that makes sense! Why didn't we think about this before?" We must move beyond the four walls of our sanctuary to care for the less fortunate in our communities. In this case, it must include the *Campesinos*.

As our evening drew to a close, I asked them what action the church could take for the *Campesinos*. Remarks such as the following came gushing forth from their mouths: "We need to show them God's love." "We need to do something for them." "We need to help them." The group was accepting their responsibility of loving their neighbor. Moreover, they were now eager to find a way to minister to the *Campesinos*.

One of the persons we discussed in the fourth lesson was César Chávez. We learned that as a Roman Catholic he utilized images such as the crucifix and *La Virgen de Guadalupe*, as well as the sacrament of Holy Communion in his leadership. He made use of the things that were familiar and held meaning to him and his people.

The study group began to vocalize how they might also use their faith to reach the *Campesinos*. As they each started to interject their ideas, they decided they would like to have an opportunity to pray for the *Campesinos* before they leave in the spring for the *piscas* in the northern states. They said, "We can have a meal for them, pray for them, give them a cross, and send them with goodie

---

5. Amos 5:23–24.

bags. Then they will know that we care for them. And maybe they won't feel so alone."

I began the fifth week by showing several movie clips from *The Harvest [La Consecha],*[6] and portions of a video on the life of Óscar Romero entitled *Romero.*[7] These film clips were very well received. The study group recalled the hard times associated with being *Campesinos*. I wouldn't say that they were embittered by their experiences. Rather, they acknowledged it was their obligation as family members to contribute to the household regardless of their age. They too had to sacrifice their happiness as children to help the *familia*. As they watched the video of whole families harvesting crops for very little money, it brought tears to their eyes. They remembered with clarity the backbreaking work, the *tijeras*, or shears, they used to cut certain produce, and the *cortito*, or short-handled hoe, that was required to harvest certain vegetables. Oh, how they dreaded that short-handled hoe! Using this tool forced them to bend over the entire day. They said just looking at the short-handled hoe made their backs hurt.[8]

With tears streaming down their cheeks, they shared stories, many of which were voiced for the first time. The stories had not been told before because they were too embarrassed by them. However, this classroom environment was a safe space. So, they spoke of their very painful sacrifices. Some gave accounts of having to sell their prized possessions just to be able to buy food for their family. The memories are still painful for them to recall. Yet, they were compelled to share because they could identify with the plight of the *Campesinos*. They understood because a part of them will always be a *Campesino*. It is almost as if it were part of their genetic material. Telling of their life experiences was therapeutic. It was cathartic for them to finally release the emotions that had for so long been deeply buried and ignored. These remembrances

---

6. Romano, *Harvest*.

7. Duigan, *Romero*.

8. The short-handled hoe was the subject of investigation for the cruel effects on farmworkers' backs. It was eventually banned by the California State Supreme Court. Jourdane, *Struggle*.

helped to deepen their gratitude to God and heighten their love and consideration for their neighbor. With each account, they thanked God for bringing them out of that life. They expressed their gratefulness to God through testimonials for the blessing of food, shelter, and clothing. By recalling their experiences, they realized their own connectedness with today's *Campesinos*. This was a watershed moment. This group had entered a new relationship with these migrant agricultural farmworkers. They no longer regarded them as "the other," or as "the stranger." No, now they were all united as *Campesinos*. They share a bond that cannot be broken. I believe by the prompting of the Holy Spirit this connection invigorated them with a greater resolve to help the migrant agricultural farmworker families.

As they watched the video of the life of Archbishop Óscar Romero they were visibly distressed. Several of them were audibly praying for him, saying such things as "Help him, Jesus." Their prayers and sentiments were so sweet and sincere. Their eyes welled up with tears as they witnessed this man of God being mistreated and finally murdered during *La Misa*. The men and women of the group exclaimed, "He was just trying to help the poor people. We need to continue to help them. We need to do our part."

The Imagine Action portion for the evening brought up some interesting stories. Several group members said, "The church needs to be present for the *Campesinos*." One of the *hermanas*, or sisters, shared a story about a baby born out in the *piscas*. The baby was stillborn. She continued saying, "There was no priest, clergy, or layperson present." The parents didn't have anyone they could reach out to for help. So, this young couple went away from the harvest fields, dug a hole, and laid their child, their baby, in the ground.

The church can do better. The church must do better in caring for this invisible group of workers. I learned as I listened to various *Campesinos*, that the death of an infant was not that uncommon. I heard various eyewitness accounts of farmworkers having to bury their own babies. Perhaps, the strenuous labor of being bent over all day and lifting heavy bushels of produce have contributed to the untimely demise of *Campesino* babies. But that research is for another time. What is in the scope of this present research is finding ways for the church to minister to the *Campesinos*. As the evening's conversation continued, the group passionately exclaimed, "We need to establish contact with them here in Seguin. Then they'll know we're praying for them and if something happens perhaps, we can help them."

In our sixth and final lesson, we reflected on the gifts that each of the exemplars we studied gave us. The gifts were the food for the evening's culmination celebration. I felt that it was appropriate to have a meal thanking God for the work of the *Campesinos*. The meal was a visual, palpable, and experiential lesson that has proven to linger in their hearts and minds long after the feast was consumed and the flavors faded from their tongues. Although the teachings occurred some time ago, I still receive comments from the group thanking me for the lessons on the *Campesinos*.

OUTCOMES

As I met with the group from La Trinidad United Methodist Church, over the course of six weeks several ideas surfaced. First, they were all in favor of offering some kind of ministry for the *Campesinos*. They were eager and enthusiastic about the prospect. There is no question that this is where their heart is at. These *hermanas y hermanos*, sisters and brothers, want to extend the love of God to their new neighbors.

Second, they need guidance and leadership in this ministry. As with most churches, the congregants look to their pastor to initiate the first steps. The pastor of our home church encouraged us to move forward without her direct involvement. Thus we learned that the success of this program is not dependent on the pastor's participation. Anyone can do this.

Third, from their healing of painful memories, the Bible study group now wants to reach out to this community. They expressed their desire to help the *Campesinos*, but they just don't know how to begin. This was a genuine transformation for this group.

Fourth, the replicable model or curriculum may be appropriated for use by other Protestant-Evangelical ministries. I hope to present this model to churches that are otherwise unaware of the presence of *Campesinos* in their community and their needs. It will also help them contextualize their faith traditions to meet the spiritual needs of migrant agricultural farmworker individuals and families.

Advocacy

It is with confidence that I say that I will be able to negotiate a meeting with the migrant agricultural farmworkers' school-aged children, their families, and some of La Trinidad's core group. I hope the Wednesday night Bible study group will be able to follow through with their dream of feeding the families and praying for them before sending them off to *el Norte*. Recently I introduced myself to the Seguin Independent School District superintendent, Dr. Matthew Gutierrez. We were attending Texas Lutheran University's National Endowment for the Arts Big Read Finale on a chilly November 12, 2022, morning in downtown Seguin. I gave the opening prayer and Dr. Gutierrez spoke of the importance of literacy, especially within his own life. As we visited briefly, I proceeded to tell him about my ministry with the *Campesinos* and the desire of the Wednesday night Bible study group to meet, feed, and pray for the families before they left in April for the *piscas*. He was very receptive to the idea of our desire to reach out to this vulnerable population. I followed up with an email to set up a date so we can meet to discuss the details. I am very thankful for this opportunity not just for the *Campesinos* or for myself, but also for the *hermanas y hermanos* of La Trinidad who want to bless these families. I firmly believe that this ministry will be a blessing to the families and the church.

My study, research, and teaching led to a second and surprising opportunity. I was invited to participate in the "2022 Leading the Way." This was a coalition of evangelical leaders from throughout the United States for the Evangelical Convening on

Immigration. This occurred in Washington, DC, on November 15th and 16th. Various groups met with their state representatives and/or staff members. I was part of a group of about ten individuals representing Texas. We had the privilege to meet with a staff member of Senator Ted Cruz's office, Liz Slezak, legislative aide. It is her responsibility to cover issues such as religion, minority issues, immigration, and women's issues to name a few.

We met at the Russell Senate Office Building in Washington, DC, where we were invited to assemble ourselves in one of the conference rooms. We began by each introducing ourselves to Liz Slezak. After this, we were each allowed to speak from our hearts on the topic that is most near and dear to us. Several spoke on issues revolving around the Dreamers. When it was my turn to speak I, of course, advocated for the *Campesinos*. As I began to speak, I reintroduced myself as a daughter and granddaughter of *Campesinos*. I shared firsthand stories of my work with the migrant agricultural farmworkers. I spoke in favor of living wages, explaining that their salary is below that of an entry-level position at the local grocery store in Seguin, Texas. The low wage is what forces children as young as the age of five to be out there harvesting alongside their parents. These children miss out on being children. I shared how a sub-par single-family apartment is outfitted to sleep four families in one bedroom. This is accomplished by hanging blankets or sheets from the ceiling to make four separate sleeping quarters. This is not adequate housing. I also asked for the restoration of dignity to this community. We need to stop treating them as though they are invisible. We need to recognize the work of their hands that we all see at the grocery stores. As important as these and many other issues that the *Campesinos* face truly are, I stated that I am also an advocate for their spiritual welfare. As a minister, it is my duty, and as Christians, it is each of our responsibility, to extend the love of God to them. All of us have access to attend a place of worship, to receive the sacraments, have our loved ones prayed for when they are sick, and be given a Christian burial when they die. No one should ever have to give birth and turn around immediately to find a place to dig a hole to bury their baby. This, I explained, is what is happening to the *Campesinos*.

I concluded my address by respectfully requesting that Senator Ted Cruz be sympathetic to the *Campesinos* and pass the Farm Workforce Modernization Act. This is a bill that will amongst other things modernize immigration for farmworkers. The proposed bill offers the following:

> Modify the method for calculating and adjusting the H-2A worker minimum wage. . . . This Bill permanently establishes the Housing Preservation and Revitalization Program, which provides financing assistance for rural rental housing and off-farm labor housing and rental assistance for qualified tenants of such housing. It also authorizes the Department of Agriculture to provide various assistance, including funding for insuring loans and grants for new farmworker housing.[9]

The proposed bill, which offers hope for the *Campesinos*, is good. Nevertheless, it does not alleviate the church's responsibility to care for them. The church cannot and should not expect our government officials to do our work for us. Spiritual matters fall into the church's domain. Nevertheless, we can work in partnership for the good of the whole person. We should toil in tandem with our government leaders.

CONCLUSION

In producing this congregational resource, I discovered that I had been training my whole life for mission and ministry with the *Campesinos*. I realize now God called me out from the *Campesinos*, from my people, to help bring the message of the saving grace of God's love to them.

Let us work to improve the quality of life and the living conditions of the *Campesinos* and then mobilize our churches to introduce Jesus Christ to these migrant agricultural workers. Let

---

9. "H.R.1603—Farm Workforce Modernization Act."

La Mesa Campesina

us use my curriculum or develop another curriculum whereby workers can be trained for the harvest. The appendices include a sample of the curriculum and helpful exhibits. Then, with great resolve let us go and meet the *Campesinos* where they are, in the fields. Jesus tells us, "The fields are ripe for harvest."[10] Therefore, we shall invite all people to God's table, to *La Mesa Campesina*.

---

10. John 4:35.

Appendix A
Jimenez Produce Truck

Photo of produce truck owned by Enrique Jimenez, maternal grandfather of Thelma Herrera Flores. Crystal City, Texas. Courtesy of Margarita J. Herrera from her personal collection.

Appendix B
Tijeras (Single Spring)

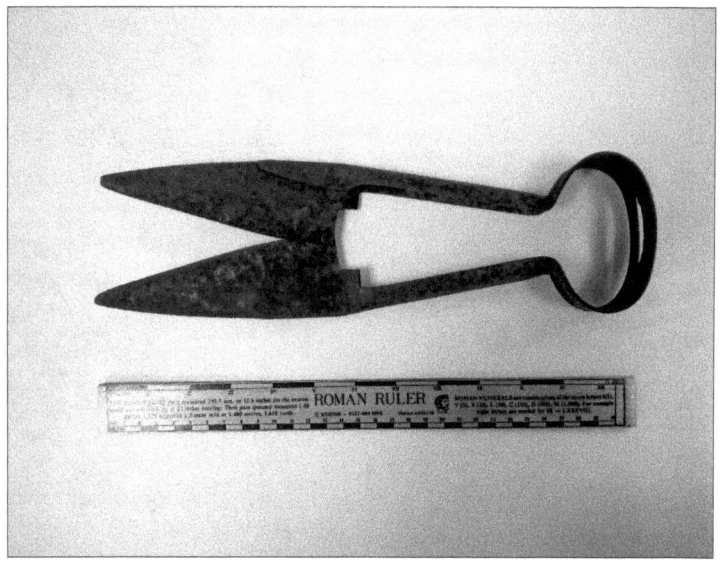

Courtesy of Margarita J. Herrera from her personal collection.

Appendix C
Tijeras (Double Spring)

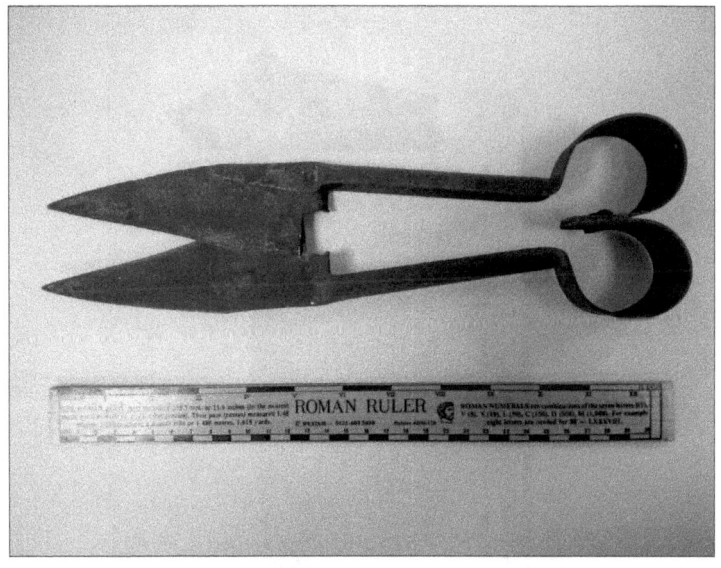

Courtesy of Miroslava V. Villarreal from her personal collection.

Appendix D
Short-Handled Hoe

Courtesy of Margarita J. Herrera from her personal collection.

Appendix E
Hand Sickle

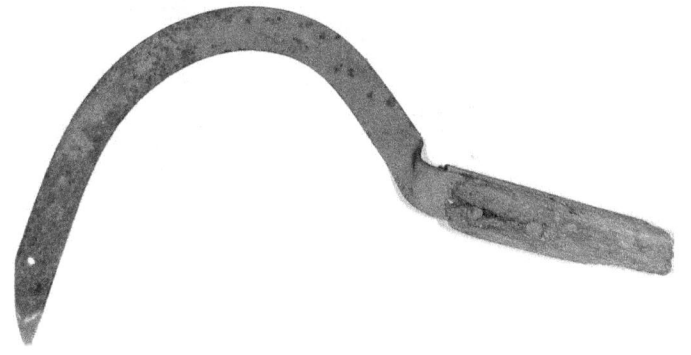

Courtesy of Ramon Alfaro from his personal collection.

Appendix F
Hand Scale

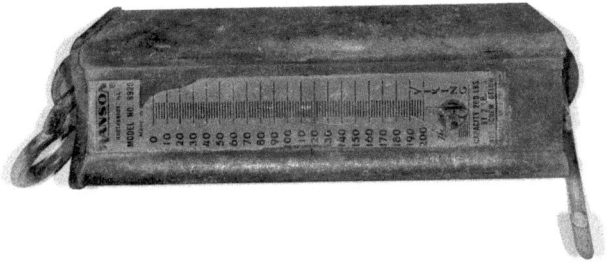

Courtesy of Margaret J. Herrera from her personal collection.

Appendix G
Popeye Statue

Popeye Statue. Pictured with Thelma Herrera Flores and her brother Joel Herrera. Crystal City, Texas, ca. 1962. Courtesy of Saul Herrera, their paternal uncle.

Appendix H
César Chávez Meeting with Hispanic Methodists in Fort Worth

Photo courtesy of Dale Woods.

Appendix I
Campesino Camp Prayer Circle

Campesino Camp Prayer Circle. Members of partner churches gathering for prayer prior to outreach ministry at Pine Acres Apartments *Campesino* housing, Ottawa County, Michigan, 2020.

Appendix J
Campesino Welcome Kit

The *Campesino* Welcome Kit included hygiene items and Spanish language Scripture portions. Assembled by Misión Holland, my ministry outreach organization for blueberry pickers in Ottawa County, Michigan.

Appendix K
"Vamos Todos al Banquete"

Vamos todos
Al banquete,
A la mesa de la creación
Cada cual, con su taburete,
Tiene un puesto y una misión.
(coro)

Hoy me levanto muy temprano,
Y me espera la comunidad;
Voy subiendo alegre la cuesta,
Voy en busca de tu amistad.

Dios invita a todos los pobres
A esta mesa común por la fe,
Donde no hay acaparadores
Y a nadie le falta el conque.

Dios nos manda hacer de este mundo
Una mesa donde haya igualdad;
Trabajando y luchando juntos,
Por el bien de la humanidad.

"Vamos Todos al Banquete / Let Us Go Now to the Banquet" from *Misa Popular Salvadoreña* by Guillermo Cuéllar, English translation by Bret Hesla and William Dexheimer Pharris.

Appendix L
Curriculum Lesson Plans

LESSON ONE: INTRODUCTION

The first meeting was used as a time to introduce ourselves to each other. I introduced myself, my topic, and the reason for my interest in this subject. In this initial meeting, I outlined my process and the duration and goal of this study. As a class, we agreed to meet from 6:00 p.m. to 7:30 p.m. each Wednesday night. The first thirty minutes, 6:00 p.m. to 6:30 p.m., were set aside for a fellowship meal with the actual study beginning promptly at 6:30 p.m. Because this is a church that enjoys singing its hymns, I proposed a song to be sung weekly. "Vamos Todos al Banquete" became our theme song. After the singing, we examined the posters from the *Bittersweet Harvest: The Bracero Program 1942–1964* exhibition, which were provided by the Smithsonian Institution Traveling Exhibition Service. Each person had an opportunity to reflect upon and comment on the images represented by the posters.

Appendix L

LESSON TWO: IDENTITY AND COMPASSION

A. Story: Moses

Read Exodus chapter 2 to understand the relationship between Moses and the Hebrew slaves.

What is the message of Exodus?

We are looking for Moses's identity and compassion but also looking for God's identity and compassion.

Who is God and what does God do for Moses and the Israelites in this portion of Scripture?

B. Group Discussion

Reflect on the experience of Moses as he moves from pharaoh's palace to the fields of Midian.

1. The Israelites suffered and were oppressed by the social system of that day.

How do these systems come into being?

How can we change them?

2. Moses's call and response are significant to the Exodus story.

Describe a time when you felt God speaking or calling you to action.

3. What is it about being a Christian that moves us to weep with those who suffer and hope with those who despair?

Appendix L

C. Imagine Action

Let's look at the story in the context of the *Campesinos*.

What actions of mission can we imagine for the local church?

Appendix L

LESSON THREE: WORK AND JUSTICE

A. Story: Amos

Homework: Read the entire book of Amos.
What are the themes of Amos?

B. Group Discussion

1. Read the following verses and identify the sins against neighbors.
    - 2:6–8
    - 4:1–3
    - 5:10–13
    - 6:4–7
    - 8:4–6
2. Read Amos 5:21–24 and answer the following question:
    What does God want from us?

C. Imagine Action

Think about the implications of Amos's story in the context of the *Campesinos*' life.

What action items can we imagine for the local church?

APPENDIX L

LESSON FOUR: *FAMILIA* AND PILGRIMAGE

A. STORY: *PIERS PLOWMAN*

William Langland believes that hard work, honest living, and charity are what will lead the pilgrim to their encounter with Truth (God). Piers equates plowing with pilgrimage.

> Said Piers, "I shall put on, then, a pilgrim's dress,
> And take you all with me until we find Truth.
> I shall put on my poor clothes all ragged and patched,
> My gaiters, and my gloves to get warmth in my fingers,
> Sling my seed bag round my neck instead of a scrip [purse],
> And bring along in it a bushel of bread-corn [grain used for making bread].
> This I myself will sow, and then soon after
> Will pilgrim-it like a palmer, in search of pardon."[1]

Piers's sowing is his pilgrimage. He will dress with palm leaves for this is how pilgrims who have visited the sacred places of the Holy Land dress.

B. Group Discussion

How does this poem or story apply to experiences of spiritual pilgrimage?

C. Imagine Action

1. What are the connections between Piers Plowman and the *Campesino* experience?

2. What can our church do to facilitate a spiritual experience for *Campesinos*?

---

1. Langland, *Piers Plowman*, passus VI.

D. César Chávez

1. What is significant about César Chávez's work ethic and belief system?

2. What were the Christian teachings/observances that he put into practice while working with the farmworkers?

E. Imagine Action

Using the information we learned from César Chávez, what can we as a church do to help the *Campesinos*?

Appendix L

LESSON FIVE: LIFE AND DEATH

A. Story: Tomás Rivera

Read the handout.

B. Group Discussion

1. What is happening in this story?
2. What is Tomás's perspective?
3. What is his mother's perspective?
4. What is the takeaway from this lesson?

C. Imagine Action

1. Is there a connection between the *Campesinos* and Tomás Rivera?

What is the connection?

2. What action can the church take to address this issue while ministering to the *Campesinos*?

D. Story: Óscar Romero

Read the handout.

E. Group Discussion

1. What are the differences between the two reading assignments?

2. What lesson can we learn from Óscar Romero that will be beneficial in our work, our dealings, and our relationships with the poor?

Appendix L

F. Imagine Action

Taking into consideration tonight's readings, what kind of action can our church take to minister to the needs of the *Campesinos*?

For Next Week's Discussion

Throughout our time together, you have heard the voices, and the alarms, and witnessed the actions of persons and characters addressing the needs of the *Campesinos*. Some of you know firsthand what their day-to-day existence is like because you, too, have experienced it. Therefore, I ask you to reflect on your own lives and think about what you wish the church had done for you.

Appendix L

LESSON SIX: *LA MESA CAMPESINA*

A. Bringing the Stories Together

We culminate our six-week journey with what I call *La Mesa Campesina*. We reflect on what each hero that we studied brings to the table. I used symbolic foods placed on what I call a *Campesina* Seder plate. This plate holds the representative offerings of the *Campesinos* as they encounter the liberating power of the gospel.

B. Liturgy: *La Mesa Campesina*

Leader:

Moses identified himself with his own people. He turned away from living a life of luxury where he could enjoy the finest food, clothing, and status to rejoin his family and his people. He worked alongside his people and chose to live with them. And he ate the food of the poor. In the case of the *Campesinos*, the common food of the poor is beans. Therefore, beans are present at our table. We acknowledge this food because this is also our food.

People: Thank you, God, for your provision!

Leader:

The hardworking Amos was a livestock breeder and a dresser of sycamore or fig trees. Amos is a good example of a migrant worker because he was from Judah in the South and God called him to go to the North to deliver God's message. Our *Campesinos* also travel from the South to the North. Amos had to go to a strange land where the people in the North knew that he was not one of them. To the table, Amos contributes lamb and figs. The lamb reminds us that Christ is our lamb, a sacrifice for our benefit.

People: For this we say, thank you, God!

Appendix L

Leader:

From Piers Plowman, we receive grain at our table. We have grain in the form of corn tortillas. Rice is also a grain, and it is present at our table in the style of Mexican rice.

People: For the humble tortillas and the rice we say, thank you, God!

Leader:

César Chávez is one of our *Campesinos*. His contribution to *La Mesa Campesina* is the fruits and vegetables that he would have harvested. Our table holds lettuce, tomatoes, and cucumbers in the form of a salad. Grapes are also present because they symbolize the struggle against injustices. Strawberries, blueberries, and pineapple in our fresh fruit salad are fruits that are also harvested by our people.

People: For these fruits and vegetables that are picked by the very young and old we say, thank you, God!

Leader:

Tomás Rivera and Óscar Romero are two very different individuals. Yet, they share food that can be hard to swallow, hot chilies and cilantro. These two foods represent for us the experience of injustice and oppression. Both items are familiar and found at almost every Mexican table. The hot chilies represent the bitter times while the cilantro introduces a certain freshness and flavor that comes with new hope.

People: For the good and the bad times represented by these foods we say, thank you, God!

Leader:

The roast chicken that is present at our table tonight is a blessing because whether we are sick or in full health it is always a blessing to have a chicken. The poor know how to make a chicken stretch. It can be roasted, boiled in a soup, or made into a *guiso* (a stew-like

Appendix L

dish). Chicken is a food that transcends status symbols. It is a dish that can be enjoyed by all.

People: And for this roasted chicken we say, thank you, God!

Leader/Prayer:

As we gaze upon and partake of each item of food let us be grateful to God not only for the food but for the calloused, rough, mahogany-colored hands that have harvested it. Our table is full to overflowing, our eyes dance with delight at the different colors, our noses are intrigued by the different aromas rising from the various dishes, and our mouths are enlivened at the prospect of sampling the delectable flavors.

All: We are a blessed people because of the *Campesinos*.

And together we say, thank you, God! Amen.

Closing Hymn: "De Colores"

This traditional Spanish folk song is a favorite of the Catholic Church and is often used during rallies and marches by the United Farm Workers Union. César Chávez and his *Campesinos* sang this song as they marched from Delano, California, to Sacramento, California. Also, Archbishop Óscar Romero in the film *Romero* can be seen sitting at a kitchen table with several nuns singing this very song. It is a joyful song that celebrates the many colors in our world.

Appendix M
Bittersweet Harvest Posters

Smithsonian Institution Traveling Exhibition Service. *Bittersweet Harvest: The Bracero Program, 1942–1964* **poster exhibition.**

Appendix N
Class Session Six

Thelma Herrera Flores teaching *La Mesa Campesina* class at La Trinidad United Methodist Church, Seguin, Texas.

Appendix O
Campesina Seder Plate

Campesina Seder plate by Thelma Herrera Flores. Clockwise from top right: lettuce, tomato, and cucumber; Mexican rice; pinto beans; grapes; figs; hot chilies; cilantro leaves. Center: corn tortilla topped with roasted lamb, used here in place of chicken, garnished with hot chilies and cilantro.

Appendix P
La Mesa Campesina Fiesta

Thelma Herrera Flores with the participants of the first cohort of *La Mesa Campesina* at their final class gathering.

Appendix Q
"De Colores"

De colores,
De colores se visten los campos en la primavera
De colores,
De colores son los pajaritos que vienen de afuera
De colores,
De colores es el arcoíris que vemos lucir

Coro:
//Y por eso los grandes amores
De muchos colores me gustan a mi//

Canta el gallo,
Canta el gallo que el quiri quiri quiri quiri quiri
La gallina,
La gallina con el cara cara cara cara cara
Los polluelos,
Los polluelos con el pío pío pío pío pío

"De Colores." Traditional Spanish folk song. Public domain.

Appendix R

H.R.1603—FARM WORKFORCE MODERNIZATION ACT OF 2021[2]

Passed House (03/18/2021.)
Farm Workforce Modernization Act of 2021

This bill contains provisions related to alien farmworkers, including provisions establishing a certified agricultural worker (CAW) status and changing the H-2A temporary worker program. The Department of Homeland Security (DHS) may grant CAW status to an applying alien who (1) performed at least 1,035 hours of agricultural labor during the two-year period prior to March 8, 2021; (2) on that date was inadmissible, deportable, or under a grant of deferred enforced departure or temporary protected status; and (3) has been continuously present in the United States from that date until receiving CAW status. The bill imposes additional crime-related inadmissibility grounds on CAW applicants and makes some other grounds inapplicable. CAW status shall be valid for 5.5 years and may be extended. DHS may grant dependent status to the spouse or children of a principal alien. An alien with a pending application may not be detained or removed by DHS and shall be authorized for employment until DHS makes a final decision on the application. A CAW alien (and dependents) may apply for lawful permanent resident status after meeting

    2. Summary quoted from "H.R.1603—Farm Workforce Modernization Act."

Appendix R

various requirements, including performing a certain amount of agricultural labor for a number of years. DHS shall create an electronic platform for (1) filing H-2A petitions, (2) facilitating the processing of H-2A cases, and (3) providing agencies a single tool for obtaining H-2A-related case information. The bill makes various changes to the H-2A program, such as (1) modifying the method for calculating and making adjustments to the H-2A worker minimum wage, (2) specifying how an employer may satisfy requirements that it attempted to recruit U.S. workers, (3) requiring H2A employers to guarantee certain minimum work hours, (4) making the program available for agricultural work that is not temporary or seasonal, and (5) reserving a visa allocation for the dairy industry. DHS shall establish a pilot program allowing certain H-2A workers to apply for portable status, which gives the worker 60 days after leaving a position to secure new employment with a registered H-2A employer. DHS shall establish an electronic system patterned on the E-Verify Program for employers to verify an individual's identity and employment authorization. Employers hiring individuals for agricultural employment must use the system. This bill permanently establishes the Housing Preservation and Revitalization Program, which provides financing assistance for rural rental housing and off-farm labor housing and rental assistance for qualified tenants of such housing. It also authorizes the Department of Agriculture to provide various assistance, including funding for insuring loans and grants for new farmworker housing.

Appendix S
Advocacy Visit to Office of US Senator Ted Cruz

Thelma Herrera Flores, National Immigration Forum advocacy visit to the office of US Senator Ted Cruz, Washington, DC, November 16, 2022.

Bibliography

Barba, Lloyd Daniel. *Sowing the Sacred: Mexican Pentecostal Farmworkers in California*. New York: Oxford University Press, 2022.

Bittersweet Harvest: The Bracero Program, 1942–1964. Poster Exhibition. Smithsonian Institution Traveling Exhibition Service. https://www.sites.si.edu/s/topic/0TO36000000ZbT9GAK/bittersweet-harvest-the-bracero-program-19421964-poster-exhibition.

Burgess, Stanley M. *The Holy Spirit: Ancient Christian Traditions*. Peabody, MA: Hendrickson, 1984.

Chávez, César. "Letter from Delano." Delano, CA: United Farm Workers Organizing Committee, AFL-CIO, 1969.

City-Data. "Seguin, Texas." City-Data.com. https://www.city-data.com/city/Seguin-Texas.html.

Conway, John S. "The Political Theology of Martin Niemöller." *German Studies Review* 9.3 (1986) 521–46. https://doi.org/10.2307/1429901.

Cuéllar, Guillermo. "Vamos Todos al Banquete / Let Us Go Now to the Banquet." From *Misa Popular Salvadoreña*. English translation by Bret Hesla and William Dexheimer Pharris. GIA Publications, 1998.

Dalton, Frederick John. *The Moral Vision of César Chávez*. Maryknoll, NY: Orbis, 2003.

"De Colores." Traditional Spanish folk song. Public domain.

Dennis, Marie, et al. *Óscar Romero: Reflections on His Life and Writings*. Maryknoll, NY: Orbis, 2000.

Duigan, John, dir. *Romero*. Paulist Pictures, TriMark Home Video, 1989. DVD.

Ferriss, Susan, and Ricardo Sandoval. *The Fight in the Fields: César Chávez and the Farmworkers Movement*. Edited by Diana Hembree. Orlando: Harcourt Brace, 1997.

"Findings from the National Agricultural Workers Survey (NAWS) 2019–2020: A Demographic and Employment Profile of United States Farmworkers." Research Report No. 16, US Department of Labor, Jan 2022. https://www.dol.gov/sites/dolgov/files/ETA/naws/pdfs/NAWS%20Research%20Report%2016.pdf.

Bibliography

Flores, Daniel F. "Faith without Walls." Sermon preached at Chapel of the Abiding Presence, Texas Lutheran University, Oct 29, 2021.

———, gen. ed. *Los Profetas: The Prophetic Role of Hispanic Churches in America*. Nashville: Wesley's Foundery, 2022.

Gadamer, Hans-Georg. *Truth and Method*. New York: Continuum, 2006.

Garcia, Maria T. *Gospel of César Chávez*. Lanham, MD: Sheed & Ward, 2007.

Gomez, Isabel. "Remembrances of La Marcha, the Farm Worker's March in Kenedy, Texas." NEA Big Read Seguin. Texas Lutheran University, Sep 24, 2022. Video of lecture. https://www.youtube.com/watch?v=lkx0LNBJ0s0.

González, Justo L. *¡Alabadle! Hispanic Christian Worship*. Nashville: Abingdon, 1996.

———. *Santa Biblia: The Bible through Hispanic Eyes*. Nashville: Abingdon, 1996.

González, Ondina E., and Justo L. González. *Christianity in Latin America: A History*. Cambridge: Cambridge University Press, 2008.

Gorman, Michael J. *Cruciformity: Paul's Narrative Spirituality of the Cross*. Grand Rapids: Eerdmans, 2001.

Gutiérrez, José Angel. *The Making of a Chicano Militant: Lessons from Cristal*. Madison, WI: University of Wisconsin Press, 1998.

"H.R.1603—Farm Workforce Modernization Act of 2021." 117th Congress (2021–2022), Mar 22, 2021. https://www.congress.gov/bill/117th-congress/house-bill/1603.

Jourdane, Maurice "Mo." *The Struggle for the Health and Legal Protection of Farm Workers: El Cortito*. Houston: Arte Público Press, 2004.

Kanter, Deborah E. "Mexican Priests and Migrant Ministry in the Midwest, 1953–1961." *U.S. Catholic Historian* 39.1 (Winter 2021) 93–112.

Keck, Leander. *The Bible in the Pulpit: The Renewal of Biblical Preaching*. Nashville: Abingdon, 1978.

Langland, William. *Piers Plowman*. Translated by Terence Tiller; general editor, Tom Griffith. Hertfordshire, UK: Wordsworth Editions, 1999.

Lyon, Drew J., and Robert N. Klein. "Estimating Winter Wheat Grain Yields." The University of Nebraska-Lincoln Extension Publications website, 2001. Revised 2007. https://extensionpublications.unl.edu/assets/html/g1429/build/g1429.htm#:~:text=thatwheat plants%2C on the, of 16%2Coookernelsperpound.

Martinez, Joel N. "La Marcha: Stories of Resilience in the 1966 Texas Farm Worker's March." NEA Big Read Seguin. Texas Lutheran University, Sep 28, 2022. Video of lecture. https://vimeo.com/753940026.

Mathews, Donald G. *Slavery and Methodism*. Princeton: Princeton University Press, 1965.

"Migrant and Seasonal Farmworker Enumeration Profiles Study—Michigan Department of Civil Rights." Michigan Department of Civil Rights (State of Michigan). https://www.michigan.gov/documents/dhs/farmworkerreport_430130_7.pdf.

Bibliography

Navarro, Armando. *The Cristal Experiment: A Chicano Struggle for Community Control.* Madison, WI: University of Wisconsin Press, 1998.

Osmer, Richard R. *Practical Theology: An Introduction.* Grand Rapids: Eerdmans, 2008.

Prifogle, Emily. "Rural Social Safety Nets for Migrant Farmworkers in Michigan, 1942–1971." *Law & Social Inquiry* 46.4 (2021) 1022–61. https://doi.org/10.1017/lsi.2021.6.

Ramírez, Gloria A. "Melon Pickers Strike of Starr County." *La Voz de Esperanza,* 50th Anniversary 29.7 (Sep 2016) 3–5.

Rivera, Tomás. *Y No se lo Tragó la Tierra . . . And the Earth Did Not Devour Him.* Houston: Arte Público Press, 1992.

Romano, U. Roberto, dir. *The Harvest [La Consecha].* Cinema Libre Studio, 2011. DVD.

Romero, Óscar. *The Scandal of Redemption.* Edited by Carolyn Kurtz. Walden, NY: Plough, 2018.

Romero, Robert Chao. *Brown Church: Five Centuries of Latina/o Social Justice, Theology and Identity.* Downers Grove, IL: InterVarsity, 2020.

Rosdahl, Bruce. "Whatever the Cost: The Formative Years of H. C. Ball, Pioneer of Hispanic Pentecostalism." *Heritage* (Jan 1, 2011) 5–13.

Russell, Jan Jarboe. *The Train to Crystal City.* New York: Scribner, 2015.

Samples, Susan. "Inside W. Mi Migrant Camps, Outreach Group Fights for Workers." WOODTV.com, Oct 7, 2020. https://www.woodtv.com/hidden-history/hispanic-heritage-month/inside-w-mi-migrant-camps-outreach-group-fights-for-workers/.

Schaff, Philip. *History of the Christian Church.* Vol. 2. Grand Rapids: Eerdmans, 1910.

Smith, Sherill. "1966 Farmworkers' Strike March Route." Hand-drawn map. Fr. Sherrill Smith collection. Archives at Archdiocese of San Antonio.

Snell, Emily. "Means of Grace: Offering Mercy, Receiving Grace." ResourceUMC, Jul 13, 2014. https://www.resourceumc.org/en/content/means-of-grace-offering-mercy-receiving-grace.

Thompson, Charles D., Jr., and Melinda F. Wiggins, eds. *The Human Cost of Food: Farmworkers' Lives, Labor, and Advocacy.* Austin: University of Texas Press, 2002.

United Methodist Church. *The Book of Discipline of the United Methodist Church.* Nashville: United Methodist Publishing House, 2016.

Villafañe, Eldin. *Beyond Cheap Grace: A Call to Radical Discipleship, Incarnation, and Justice.* Grand Rapids: Eerdmans, 2006.

Wesley, John. *The Bicentennial Edition of The Works of John Wesley.* Vol. 3, Sermons III. Edited by Albert Outler. Nashville: Abingdon, 1986.

White, James. *Sacraments as God's Self Giving.* Nashville: Abingdon, 1983.

www.ingramcontent.com/pod-product-compliance
Lightning Source LLC
Chambersburg PA
CBHW071623170426
43195CB00038B/2040